My Opinion

Just Some Thoughts

KARA MORE

PAGE PUBLISHING, INC.
Conneaut Lake, PA

First originally published by Page Publishing 2020

ISBN 978-1-6624-0314-9 (pbk)
ISBN 978-1-6624-0315-6 (digital)

Printed in the United States of America

Introduction

I'm an opinionated person, and I like to analyze everything that happens. It might be the Irish in me to give opinions on just about everything because I've been this way since I can remember. This is why I've decided to write a book on current social and political issues. Since I'm not a person who studies history, my opinions will be my own thoughts and conclusions with maybe a hint of history. Of course, everyone has their own opinions, and I respect the fact that their opinion may or may not agree with mine. But I have learned that I can always learn from reading or listening to others opinions. That doesn't mean I'll change my opinion, but there are times that I have benefited from others' opinions. This open-minded way of thinking has given me a different way of thinking about a specific subject, but it doesn't change my values or my understanding of right and wrong. My opinion may not always be accurate or make sense to others. Hopefully, people will think about each opinion before they toss them aside. Maybe my opinion will encourage people to ask a friend or themselves what they think and may even create questions for a good debate, or even change a person's opinion. I'm hoping that people who read my opinions will not reject them because of their emotions, but rather, I hope that they think about what I've said and keep an open mind before they decide whether they accept or disagree with that opinion.

I find it quite interesting that people have so many diverse ways of presenting various ideas and topics of interest about different species, ecosystems, stars, moons, planets, atmospheric makeups, and that humans all have their own DNA. That's why I believe that listening and understanding different people's idea is so fascinating and helps me process all environmental input. Thinking about others' opinions helps me decide and come up with a better conclusion from which I base my opinions. Does that mean that my opinions are written in stone? No. But it would take someone who can prove to me that their thinking is logical, fair, reasonable, and thoughtful with examples or other materials from which they base that opinion. Of course, I'm always open to constructive criticism and debate about any subject manner that pertains to my opinions because I believe that's how we learn and make things better for ourselves and society as a whole.

When reading my opinions, it will be great if you take in consideration that I am not perfect and may need rebuked, but you should keep in mind that everyone deserves a certain level of respect instead of hateful threatening rhetoric that only serves to create divisions. I believe that one can have an opinion without making judgements or condemning that person as an individual. My belief is that everyone has the right to believe and live as they see fit as long as they aren't harming someone else in the process. Of course, today's standards of harming others has such a low bar that if you sneeze, that's considered harmful to some. There are some things that I write about that will probably offend others, but I'm not trying to shame or judge people's souls. This is true even if I don't agree with their behaviors, or have the same beliefs. My moral compass doesn't allow me to judge others that don't think the same as I think. What I do believe is that I should respect the fact that others should be respected as fellow human beings. Anyway, I hope readers will find this book quite unique and easy to think about, but reality tells me that there will always be critiques that people just can't agree, which is okay. But I will not entertain or accept hateful threats or rhetoric that some will want to direct toward my opinions. Nor will I accept being called a bigot just because a person disagrees with my opinions.

Abortion

Some women say that abortion is their right and their decision to determine what happens to their own body. Others say it's wrong and at best should happen before there is a fetal heartbeat. Well, I believe that this is a very serious matter to think about and to discuss the matter in an objective way that looks at what constitutes a living being, what are the alternatives, what I personally believe, and what are the effects on the mother, baby, and the abortionist. I want to make it clear that I'm not writing to judge people, but rather, to state what I think and argue at what point that the fertilized zygote becomes a living being. Also, I'll make a few personal comments that might be noteworthy to some and offensive to others.

It seems obvious that without a heartbeat, no one is alive, and a living human being will continue to live only if the heart keeps beating. I don't believe anyone can deny or argue against that fact. Therefore, a baby is a living being once a heartbeat is detected. If it's a human that's carrying the embryo, then it's a human being. I believe that once the fetus has a heartbeat, then not only does that constitute a living being, but it also means that the fetus has a soul. I suggest this because by the end of the first trimester, the baby has all the parts needed to live outside the mother. Of course, the baby's body needs more time to mature so that they can breathe and survive outside the womb. Of course, all baby animals need a mother to protect them and to teach them how to live in a world that has many obstacles to overcome. This is no different from a child that cannot live by themselves when they are under the age of ten or younger because they don't have the maturity to make decisions or experience that adults understand is important. Most people wouldn't expect a five-year-old to get a job and pay their own bills because reasonable people understand that children don't have the ability to live on their own. Children under sixteen still need a parent to protect them and to make decisions for them. Does that make that child less of a human?

Another school of thought is that you can't say that the heart is beating because the fetus isn't anything but a clump of cells and doesn't become a human until it's born. Well, with that thinking, I can say that we are all just a bigger clump of cells, and I was just lucky that my mom decided to give birth to my clump of cells. As you can tell, I don't believe this argument holds water, or is an argument that most reasonable people would or could actually agree that it's a valid argument. But if someone wants to convince themselves that they are right far be it from me to try to convince them that a heartbeat indicts life regardless of what or from where it comes. Again, I believe that not only are we just a clump of cells with a heartbeat, but we also have the ability to live outside the womb and become people who are capable of doing great things that benefit others.

It's sad to me that women don't see that a child can be a blessing instead of an inconvenience that they can just throw in the trash. Maybe they should decide that motherhood isn't for them and just get their tubes tied so that they can't get pregnant. But others might think about discussing with a doctor, which birth control that is proven to prevent 99 percent of pregnancies and one that they don't have to remember to take. Now that is a sure way that women can control their bodies and still feel a sense of having control over their bodies. Many women use birth control for this very reason, and they can still have children at a later date of their choosing to become a mom. Of course, only if that's what they want for their future. After all, if you decide you just don't want to be a mother, then there is nothing wrong with not being a mother. I also believe that the morning-after pill is a form of birth control, but others believe that the morning-after pill is just another way to destroy a potential baby. This simply isn't the case because if I remember correctly, it takes a while for the sperm to reach the egg; therefore, if taken within twelve hours, then it's more of a birth control method.

Again, there is nothing wrong if a woman decides not to have children, but to use abortion as a means for birth control seems a bit extreme and unnecessary given the information about birth control options that can be obtained easily, and most birth control methods are affordable. I'm sure that in this day and age that there are plenty of options and choices regarding both obtaining various birth control methods and not have to worry about the cost. After all, abortions are medical procedures that are provided for people who don't have insurance. It seems that using birth control is safer. Also, I believe that even most prochoice people recognize that when any person goes through any type of medical procedure, there are possible risk factors involved.

Again, there should be no shame in deciding not to become a parent. I believe that becoming a parent should be between the woman and the man. It might be the women's body, but because men are part of the process of making a baby, then they should be part of the decision-making process. All the decision-making about parenting ideally is discussed before impregnation takes place, but we're living in a different time. It's important to make sure that birth control is discussed before you engage in sex so that there is no need to even think about abortion. A woman shouldn't let anyone make them feel bad about their decision not to become a mother. My thoughts are is that other people may complain about you not wanting to have a child, but it's the mother who usually adjusts her life to meet the needs of the children. It's the women who know whether they have the ability to put a child's needs before their own. But the women who use abortion as a birth control method might want to seriously think about sterilization because I believe they and the child would be better off. Just some thoughts.

Next, I think it's important to think about the after effects of an abortion that may or may not affect the mother or the person performing the abortion. But if someone decides to have or perform an abortion, I think that it's important for all involved to understand what the consequences might occur while and after an abortion. If the baby has their arm torn off and survives the abortion, I would think it would be forever burned into the minds of the woman and the abortionist. I can't even imagine how anyone can think it's okay to rip a baby apart just so a woman has control over her body. It seems to me they should maybe think about controlling their actions before they get stuck with an unwanted baby. It just makes me sick just thinking about the pain the baby has just experienced. Also, don't try to tell me that babies don't feel pain before birth. Just for the fact that they have a nervous system should tell you that they can feel pain. It always amazed me how people can justify any decision when they don't want to look at the problems that result from engaging in various behaviors.

One of the biggest problems or aspect of getting an abortion is the emotional toll it can have on the woman. I understand that a lot of women don't realize the emotional and mental complications that can take place after an abortion, but they should think long and hard about what the consequences might be if they decide to follow through with an abortion. I've never had an abortion, but I've known women who did, and they usually live with guilt that never totally goes away. Sometimes the guilt can be overwhelming, and the woman never gets over the guilt. This can lead to depression that keeps them from forgiving themselves. Really, it takes strong women to forgive themselves and for them to overcome such guilt, and this can affect how she views her future as a mother. I remember a friend of mine who was struggling with her spiritual life because she had two abortions but was ready to and wanted to be a mom. She struggled with self-doubt, with depression, and felt that God wasn't blessing her with children because of those two abortions. I felt bad for her, but I didn't really know what to say to help her because I didn't believe in abortions, nor did I ever resort to abortions. But I didn't judge her or stopped being her friend. She now has three children, loves being a mom, and can help others who face the same dilemma. I'm sure she probably still has days that she experiences guilt and wonder what might have been if she had decided not to have those abortions. I just don't believe in scolding anyone about their behaviors because I'm too busy trying to make sure I do what's right.

Another aspect of an abortion to consider is the person who is performing the abortion. I've tried to put myself in the shoes of the woman who has the abortion, and I can somewhat understand the reasoning for their choice, but for the life of me I can't imagine how anyone performing an abortion after the heartbeat becomes noticeable and just throws the baby into a container like trash or just a piece of rotten food. It seems to me that to be able to continue performing abortions, they would have to be able to compartmentalize what they saw and what they did to a living being. Otherwise, how can they live with themselves and go home to their families and believe that it's not wrong? Personally, I believe if you can kill a baby, you probably could kill anyone who you decide is a problem. Also, the government should never be able to force any person to go against their conscience by forcing or mandating that they perform an abortion. Since the woman has a choice about having an abortion, then it's only fair that the health-care worker has the choice to refuse to perform the abortion.

Next, anyone who decides to let a full-term baby die, or assist in their death, is only lying to themselves that it's the mother's right. I believe that a woman who can carry a baby for nine months and can decide to let the baby die or be executed should never have any more children because in my opinion, they probably aren't mother material. Again, I'm not judging anyone. I'm just saying it would be better not to have children if you don't see that they are little human beings that need a mom to protect them, not order their execution. Just some thoughts.

America Home of the Free

There is no definition in the dictionary for describing what America means to me, but if you ask a patriot, you will hear things like the constitution, freedom, home of the brave, opportunity, rule of law, limited government, democracy, republic, capitalists, and apple pie. This is just a few of the words or phrases that help define what most patriotic people think that America represents. On the other side of our society, you hear things like oppression, bigots, only the wealthy and the whites have privileges, cops and laws are against minorities, and Americans don't care about other nations. Well, let me tell you what I think about America and people's attitudes.

First, I want to recognize and make it clear that I am not sure why some people in the beginning of this great nation felt like they needed slaves, but I don't believe that I can judge them because I didn't exist at that time. Also, when people write history, they usually see it through their perspective. It's easy to condemn someone else, but I prefer to not judge others. I also realize that there were evil people back then as there are evil people today. I think it's a safe bet that there were probably good people back then that cared about others. There will always be good and evil in this world because people can be capable of both behaviors. It would be a sure bet that people always experience both good and evil. This has been true in the past, it is true today, and will without a doubt be true about people until the end of time. This fact doesn't make it right, but you cannot refute the fact that all cultures have their share of evil people. So with this in mind, please read what I have to say with an open mind because I do not hate or judge others because of their being or their beliefs. But I do pick and choose who my friends are regardless of skin color. Also, I don't hang around people who have beliefs and behaviors that are so different from mine. Another thing, I don't like to be around people who want to try and argue philosophy. It's not because I don't like to question spiritual events, rather, it's hard to explain my experience because you can't prove or disprove most spiritual events, nor is it easy for someone else to understand something that they haven't experienced themselves, and it's just futile to try. Of course, I do not associate with evil people because to me, they might be capable of doing much harm to me or my loved ones. So with that said, let me expand on what I believe might help people get along and be more respectful of themselves and others. Just some thoughts.

America is the land of opportunity, if you're willing to sacrifice and work hard. It is a place where you can advance and become the person you want to become if you work hard and keep a positive attitude. It's easy to think negative and get bogged down with what you see or believe is holding you back. Of course, there are difficulties and obstacles that can seem almost impossible to solve but don't let yourself give in to blaming others. My brother Doug would say, "People are poor because poor people have poor ways." I agree with that because even people who have physical and mental disabilities have overcome them by looking at possibilities instead of choosing to dwell on or what they perceive as hopeless due to circumstances beyond their control. Although I can't fully understand what it is like to be black, I can understand what people go through when others think that you are not good enough to be part of society. You see, when I was a child, other kids at school and some adults treated me very badly. They also bullied me and even shamed me in front of my classmates, all because I was poor. I never hated them for what they did, instead, I just associated with the two friends who wanted to be my friends. It is hard now for me to understand why these two girls befriended me because both of them came from wealthy families. Of course, this experience has stayed with me all my life. I don't blame people for their ignorance or judge them because they have more material things than I do. Instead, I choose to work and focus on what I believe makes me a better person. So the bottom line is I don't let others control my thoughts, actions, or how I treat people of different backgrounds.

There are many lessons that a person learns from living in poverty, and these lessons have both positive and negative ways that you view others. I've learned that the lack of or the abundance of money doesn't make you a good or bad person. A person's income level has little to do with your importance because every person is made in God's image and therefore is important. To me, I've been blessed to be born in America. Being an American gives people hope and the opportunity to succeed if they work hard enough toward that goal. What some people don't realize or understand is that even poor people in this country live better than the poverty that my family experienced. How many people on government assistance go to bed or school hungry? How many don't have indoor plumbing or even shampoo to wash their hair? How many of these people have had to eat thistle greens because of no money to buy food? Just a note: I'm not talking about people who sell food stamps for drugs, I'm talking about the men and women who do work but either choose to keep the government out of their lives, or just make a little too much money to qualify for assistance. Also, there are people all over the world that experience this and worse. This is why I have such a hard time with people in this country who complain about America. How sad is that?

Next, America is a place that you can feel safe because we are a nation of laws. Although there are some areas that are getting worse in bigger cities, I believe that most people would agree that overall, America is one of the safest places to live. There are many factors that keep or make areas of America more dangerous to raise a family, some of which I will, or at least attempt, to discuss in various other opinions. But overall, compared to the 1800s, most people can live their life without feeling danger.

Another issue that is of concern to me is when people burn the flag or talk about how horrible and unfair that they are treated. I'm not sure why people who say any bad or degrading things about America still want to stay. They have every right to leave, but they might have a hard time finding another country where you can burn their flag. I'm sure that someone would be more than happy to assist them with a one-way ticket to their preferred choice of countries.

They could maybe ask others who might be willing to provide them a one-way plane ticket to their chosen destination with the stipulation that to come back into this country, they would have to get in line and apply for citizenship. Something tells me they would want to work so that they can get back to this country. Also, they would probably be begging and taking people to court to get their citizenship restored. Just some thoughts.

I believe that most Americans just want to live their lives in a free, safe, and peaceful environment where they can keep themselves and their loved ones safe and happy. Most people just want to be able to work and pay a fair tax so that they can save their money or spend their money the way they choose. Working people like to make enough money so that they can save money and have money for things that they enjoy. Most people live and let live, but there are some people who I call the malcontents. Malcontents are usually troublemakers that are unhappy and can't stand that you are happy. They blame all their misery and problems on others instead of looking at their own behaviors. These people usually look at successful people and blame the rich for not sharing it with them and others. Tell me one good reason why I should have to give my money to support others or make the politicians rich. I think it was nice for someone to help me, but I didn't think that I should make people help me or give me money. Just a note. You hear some politician say that it's the Christian thing to help the needy. But Jesus didn't command people to help others. He did suggest that each person would be blessed for being kind and giving strangers a drink of water. Jesus did command that we should not bare false witness against others. I think it's good to help others, but sometimes helping others just feeds into their lazy or dysfunctional behaviors. Also, the Bible doesn't suggest that the government has the right to steal hardworking, successful people's money so that they and others can benefit. But the Bible, if I remember correctly, does mention that each person who is able bodied should work, or they should go hungry. So don't try to tell me that I should give a lazy person a part of the fruits of my labor. There are those who I do believe need our help and compassion. These are folks who, for no cause of their own, aren't able to take care of themselves—people who are developmental delayed and people like the elderly that are no longer able to work. I believe that we are a blessed nation because who will and does help the ones who are the least among us. In my opinion, caring of others who can't take care of themselves is just one of the reasons why God has blessed this great nation that we call America. Just some thoughts.

Climate Change
Real or Not Real

Today, instead of teaching kids about photosynthesis, children are being indoctrinated in the evil of climate change. They are told how carbon dioxide and cows are going to end our lives if we don't change our ways and get rid of fossil fuels. This thinking does nothing for adults or children, except maybe make them neurotic and fearful. The government and climate activists do this so that they can get people on the bandwagon of their agenda. They want every person but themselves to stop using fossil fuels. People like Al Gore really don't believe that carbon is causing the Earth to warm too much because he has a bigger carbon footprint by how he conducts his own life. Just look at his behavior. Oh wait, maybe this rule applies to just the elite and the rest of us should just be thankful that these so-called intelligent people will allow us to even exist, or maybe not? After all, we do emit carbon dioxide every time we exhale.

It's obvious that there is a driven agenda by how so-called elite intellectuals use climate change to explain or blame every problem that occurs in the universe. This indicates their scientific methodology is flawed. Also, they don't really know for sure whether it's climate change or global warming. Who knows what the next label will be to try and convince people of their thinking. From what I can tell and from what I know from analyzing and reasoning about climate change is that there is a lot more questions than answers for why some people believe that climate change is real. It is my opinion that the so-called elite intellectuals should ask themselves and should study their hypothesis or little project with more in-depth thinking. It seems to me that they change their stance on what defines climate change, and they keep moving the goalpost on when we will die from lack of clean air.

The latest reason for concern is the severity of the weather. Well, I've been alive long enough to see that the weather gets milder some years and then for whatever reason, it goes back to being more severe. If climate change was based on pure scientific research, then it should be objective. There should be no room to keep guessing every time the wind blows a different direction. One conclusion I have come to about this political scare tactic is that whoever did this research left a lot of reasons in why people should question their scientific methods. I personally cannot see how they scientifically determined that carbon dioxide and cows are dangerous to our lives. What seems an absolute truth about these scientists when analyzing their results is that these scientist didn't do a very thorough analysis. Therefore, I'm left with the conclusion that they don't know what they are talking about, or they are just political hacks that are using scare tactics. Therefore, they have an agenda of their own making.

Here are some questions that I would like answered. Why or how do you know that the carbon dioxide on Earth is the cause for this change? Why do you believe that the hole in the ozone layer is due to human behavior instead of maybe a meteor emitting a gas as it denigrates into our atmosphere? What would happen to our air quality if there were no cows? How much carbon dioxide is needed in order for plant life to continue and produce oxygen for all life to maintain existence? Why do you pick on just cows? It's my understanding that any animal with a complex digestive system emits gas from one end and carbon from the other. What makes you think that cows aren't important, and cows may even be the necessary source of nitrogen that is a big part of the air we breathe? I could come up with other questions, but I think most will understand where I'm going with these questions.

To better understand the issue of the greenhouse effect would take too long, so my focus on climate change will be on what I understand. Therefore, I will start with discussing the basic facts about photosynthesis and how carbon dioxide and nitric oxide plays important roles for our existence. Hopefully, in doing this, it will help explain the whole process of how carbon dioxide helps plants and humans. Also, I want to talk some about why cows are important as I believe every life-form is important and contributes to our survival as a species. I'm going to look at and ask some more questions that I believe are valuable and might help with understanding the good as well as the bad results that are possible if we decide to limit carbon and other gases.

Let's begin with some facts. There are four different seasons that most places on planet Earth experience during 365 days a year. Different countries have different climates and environmental conditions that people cannot change. Green plants for sure have to have carbon dioxide to kick-start photosynthesis that produces oxygen in our atmosphere, and without carbon dioxide and sunlight, photosynthesis wouldn't take place, and therefore, plants couldn't produce oxygen. What would happen to life on Earth if plants didn't produce enough oxygen? Next, cows seem to be enemy number two of climate change. Well, let's look at how cows benefit life. Cows provide nitrogen-rich fertilizer that helps provide the soil with the necessary nutrients that aids the farmers in producing food for our health and well-being. I'm not sure, but again, it seems to me that the nitrogen produced by cattle might be the source of nitrogen that is a necessary component of the air we breathe. What would happen to our atmosphere air quality if we didn't have cattle? What would happen to plants and the air if they didn't get enough carbon dioxide? Just some thoughts.

The problem I believe starts with people who like to believe and want to have control over others and various situations. One thing I can tell you is that the older I get, the more I realize that I have very little control over events or life itself. Another fact is what I do or don't do has little or no influence on weather patterns or any other natural disasters. If scientists are really concerned about the reasons why such severe weather occurs, then maybe they should study things like the effects of nuclear test blasts, or maybe how manufacturing man-made snow affects the environment. What I believe is that God's creation or nature's creation, whichever one you believe, has only positive results, but when people think they can do better at creation, then there's usually a flawed end product. I also believe that any time humans get involved with trying to improve our lives by artificial means usually doesn't do a better job but actually does more harm.

The next fact is every aspect of life is in a constant stage of changing and that includes rocks and dirt. How and why that happens is somewhat known by scientist who study geology and other sciences, but not everything is fully understood about any life or other events in life. Some may argue that about evolution or creation, but I find it hard to dispute that everything has a purpose. Also, plants and other life are interdependent on each other for survival. Again, I ask, has anyone even asked or studied the effects on life when there is no carbon dioxide in the atmosphere. One of the observations that I have determined is when there is less plant life, there is less oxygen. Just think about the higher elevations over a certain point: less vegetation seems to indicate that there is a correlation with when there is less vegetation, then there is less oxygen.

Listen, I'm all for making life better for all life, but don't just drop ideas without looking at the whole picture and the consequences. When changing what has worked for hundreds of years, I believe it is important to analyze what the negative effects or dangers might be when people try to improve on nature or God's creation. Cows are here for a reason, and they are not the only animals that put methane into the atmosphere. When any time that studies just pick one subject from many that produce methane gas, then this indicates to me that it isn't about methane. Therefore, it seems to be more about the cattle industry and politics than it is about reality. In fact, I would more likely believe that renewable energy was for protecting life if Al Gore gave up all conveniences and lead by example. No one needs a private jet, which puts out carbon in the atmosphere where there are no plants to absorb the carbon. Who really needs more than two homes, which doubles their carbon footprint? Of course, it shouldn't be up to me to tell someone else how to live, but if you're going to make a believable argument about so-called climate change, then you should live as if your behavior reflects those beliefs. Even though jets put out a lot of carbon dioxide, I think this still would not make a big difference to the atmosphere. The reason I believe that carbon dioxide wouldn't affect our atmosphere is because most gases disperse as it rises, and as gasses rise up into the atmosphere, it's doubtful that it could even reach the ozone layer. Also, the universe is so endless that carbon dioxide couldn't possibly have much effect on the environment, but the lack of carbon dioxide does affect photosynthesis. It seems to me that it might be reasonable to conclude or believe that it is next to impossible for carbon dioxide here on Earth to have any significant role in the weather or anything else except photosynthesis. What really is hard to believe is that cows are the problem. What about other animals that emit methane gas? I'm just not convinced. There are just too many unanswered questions. Just some thoughts.

Another aspect that needs to be considered. When people exercise, do they put out more carbon? If so, does that mean we should outlaw people who exercise? As you might be thinking that there is no end on what might be producing unnecessary carbon, you might also ask, who's this benefiting? Like everything that the government does or tries to control is usually to help those in power. I do believe if some people in government can figure out how to tax people for the amount of oxygen we use, we will all have to pay more taxes or maybe they would cut off our oxygen. I'm not convinced that there are serious scientists that have studied climate change that actually are serious about believing that people and cows can actually control bad weather.

Another fact is everything that exits goes through changes that may or may not be to our liking. Our cells are constantly changing, and if we live long enough, every time we look into a mirror, it helps us face that reality. It would be nice if someone invented a pill that could stop the results of aging, you bet, but what is the downside or side effects? Even after death, there is a change that takes place and is normal. When we die, the body will start to decay, and the only way we can control this decay from taking place is to cremate or embalm the body. Otherwise, we have no control over the decaying of the physical body.

I believe that there are only two reasons that powerful people have when they start agendas like climate change. Either they have too much time on their hands, or they think they are so much smarter than the other people in this country. They actual believe that they are doing the rest of us a favor. After all, they think we are so helpless and stupid. (By the way, this is the textbook definition of self-importance.) Why do they think it's their job to make sure that we have no right to disagree, or why they want to make a law to make climate change real? After all, they were educated at Harvard! I get sick of hearing that phrase because I've known people who have a better understanding about issues that didn't even finish high school. God help us if another Harvard graduate gets to be the next president. Just one last thought. Some people believe that climate change is an existential threat to life on Earth. Instead of climate change being an existential threat to life on Earth, I believe that toxic stupidity represents more of an existential threat to our existence as a free nation than climate change. Something to think about. Just some thoughts.

Equality: Fact, Fiction, or Otherwise

Wouldn't it be wonderful if being equal were true? But nothing is perfectly equal, not even two cups of water. Just think about people. Some people are better-looking than others, while others have a hard time with being told that they are just attractive. I wish I could sing like Celine Dion, but I can't even get close. In fact, one time I was singing, it must have hurt my dog's ears because he started howling. Also, some people don't have families that are supportive, or their families don't even want to be part of their lives anymore. Where is the fairness about any of that? Of course, everyone should have a fair chance at developing into who they want to be, but most people need to have certain abilities or education in order to qualify for certain jobs. Intellectual and physical abilities usually play a part in various workplace environments. I wished I could get a job with developing computer programs, but I have a hard time knowing how to send e-mails. Does that mean that I'm stupid? No, but what it tells me is that I don't have the skills or the knowledge, or maybe I just don't have the necessary abilities that are required.

With all that said, let's look at some of the social inequalities that people suggest exists and maybe some suggestions on how to better life. Certainly, there was a time that people of color were disadvantaged in numerous social settings but that doesn't seem to be the biggest problem today. Of course, not everyone is going to like you, or they may be bigots, but most people today realize that skin color isn't the criteria to base the worth of others. Instead, I believe that the attitudes of some people regardless of color seem to be what is problematic. Some people just maintain an attitude of helplessness, which gives them a victim status that benefits them. I believe some people don't really want to be equal, and this includes people who are not minorities. They want to be considered special, and they shouldn't have to play by the same rule book, and they believe that they can do whatever it takes to make sure others are miserable too. This makes me think what they really want is to be able to get special treatment not equality. Of course, this dependent behavior is rewarded in our society today, and most people are satisfied with getting on government assistance. One of the ways that they use to manipulate others is to point the finger at people who are successful in order to justify their circumstances.

The main problem with thinking that others are causing the unfair treatment is a person can't focus on how they can help themselves. Folks, there was a time when people in America did just fine without government intervention. People at one time had to solve problems on their own, but today, the government makes it hard to live without their help, and therefore, the government feeds into this self-perceived helplessness. This also gives them a reason for blaming the rich or the privileged whites. When people see themselves as victims, then they don't have the incentive to work because it's just easier to blame someone else for their circumstances, and this thinking is being reinforced by a big segment of our society. It's as if people think that being equal is just another excuse that blinds them and keeps them a victim. I believe that when you are dependent on someone else, or the government, then you become their property. Therefore, you have become a victim of your own making by your own self prophecy. Just some thoughts.

Another way that some people keep their victim status is to use the race or the gender card. You might hear such phrases as "Minorities are denied equal opportunities because of white privilege" or "Because I'm poor, or because I'm a woman, I'm treated differently on the job." Another popular excuse among blacks is that "My ancestors were enslaved, and because of this, I feel oppressed." Another popular excuse is "I'm not going to do slave labor because whites owe me reparations for enslaving my ancestors." You'll hear women complain about that they aren't treated like men. It seems to me that their ancestors weren't the only slave in their lives. The biggest slave in their lives is being kept slaves by their own thinking and holding on to their excuses for not helping themselves. Other excuses you hear is they can't find a job because they went to bad schools. Another reason is that whites, especially white men, have always had more privileges. Women like to use the excuse that men are more likely to be in leadership roles. On the other hand, a lot of women will use their sex as a weapon against men. You don't hear men complaining about a woman harassing them. Why not just prove that you can be a leader and wait for a job opening and apply for a leadership position?

Some more thoughts about equality and being a victim. Do you really think that fighting the Civil War was a privilege? Do you think that there was more white men who were killed? If you said yes to that question, then you would be correct because most Civil War soldiers were white. They did this because they didn't think other people should be owned and be forced to feel and be treated like they were less of a human being. Winning the Civil War created a path for blacks to enjoy freedom and to exercise their God-given rights to live out their dreams. Of course, the blacks still faced monumental difficulties and were treated worse than other people. This mistreatment lasted well into the twentieth century, but at what point does a person stop blaming others? The same concept includes women complaining about their rights. At what point will women feel that they have equal rights? It seems that people who claim to be victims will never stop complaining because it's just too easy and popular in our society to blame others and to remain a victim. You see, I believe that it's human nature to keep taking and using unless you decide it's wrong. In this day and age in America, you don't have to forever continue to be a victim. Why not just look at the positive attributes of your fellow Americans and join the rest of us who struggle to make our lives better every day? Just some thoughts.

Maybe it might help others to move past some of their thinking if they look at what they think or consider is privilege. Also, it might help take the focus off themselves and think about other people's struggles. First, you need to get the focus off yourselves and try to understand that every person on this planet struggles with something in their lives that they can't change. It's hard for any person when the only thing they can do is to accept the situation, or just be happy it isn't something worse. If you can't or aren't willing to try and change, then you need to just accept your circumstances. Personally, I have several things in my life that I would like to change. There are some that I have control over, and there are some things I don't have control over. I can't change a lot in my life that I feel isn't fair, but I can look at the positive capabilities in my life and be thankful. It could have been much worse. Another way to think about other people's struggles is to ask yourself what you would do if you had the chance to go into a room to leave your cross that you bare and exchange it for another? Do you think you'd want to take it back for the one you had before? It's been something I've thought about over the years.

Next, there are many people who believe that if they only had more money, or if everyone got paid equal pay, then their lives would be better. I'm just as guilty as the next person when it comes to thinking that money is the answer to people's problems. So let's examine how money may or may not help improve a person's life. Money doesn't buy your health, it doesn't buy you true love, it doesn't buy you loyal friends, it doesn't make you a better person, and you can't take it with you when you die. The only thing that money helps with is material needs and maybe helps with stress levels if you could afford to go on vacations. Some of the bad things that all too often occur is that money usually changes people for the worst, like they think they can buy love, loyalty, friendships, etc. Some people think they are so powerful that they use their money to buy status, or to cover up for wrongdoing. News flash: you really only temporarily benefit from stolen money, and money can't get you to heaven. It's better to have a little and be humble than to be rich and think you don't have to play by the same rules. My belief is that the more blessings you are given, the more is expected of you to help others. This doesn't mean that the government has the right to demand or dictate what you do with your money. God wants each of us to give of ourselves from the heart, not out of duty. Last, when you have money, everyone thinks you owe them, and they use you as a scapegoat for their problems. Just some thoughts.

Let's look at poverty. There is even an upside from being raised in poverty and enduring hardships of many forms. First, it helps to look at the strengths you possess due to being raised in poverty and the positive lessons you learned from the unfair and abusive treatment you have endured just because your skin color is different, or you live in situations that are beyond your control. As a child, I wasn't in control of my life and couldn't do much about anything. Being born into a family that had less material things than others is just one example, but now that I'm an adult, I'm capable in making my own choices, and I live in a great country where I have the right to change things, or just accept what I can't change.

Since I know firsthand about growing up in poverty, I can share some thoughts and ideas that may help others. I must say that I didn't even know that I was poor until someone pointed that out to me once I started school. Then I learned that I wasn't as good as other people, and I was told that at least once a day at school. There were no adults that told the kids to stop being mean. I just grew up thinking that I wasn't a good person. So please understand that being a minority isn't the only way to understand being treated badly. I believe in forgiveness and not letting the past define who I am. I still fall back into wishful thinking and regrets, but overall, I get up each day being thankful for what I have in my life. It's not easy, but at least I'm not acting like a victim and blaming others. Instead of dwelling on all the bad in your life, you can focus on those hardships and how everything in life will either make you a stronger and better person, or it will make you a weak and an ineffective victim. Also, instead of becoming cruel and hateful like the ones you blame, learn how to overcome or deal with life's trials and obstacles in positive ways. Although living in poverty presents various struggles, disappointments, failures, and hardships in my life. I have been able to overcome these obstacles and have learned what one must do in order to rise above negativity, and I have learned instead to dwell on the positives. Instead of hating someone for their success, I want to learn more about how they got to be successful.

I understand that blacks have been pushed aside in the past but to continually demonize all white people for the injustices is a pathway to becoming just as evil as the person that you hate. My way of making sense of hurt and anger is to consider how not forgiving others only affects you more than the person who you hate. Instead, I look at the people who harmed me as pitiful people who I don't want or need in my life. I tell myself that if I continue hating them, then I might become just like them or worse. I sure don't want to treat anyone like I was treated especially if there is a chance that I might become like them. Just some thoughts.

The last area that I want to comment about is the workplace. When you work for someone, that person has every right to expect people to give 100 percent to doing the best job while they are at work. What you receive for your work should be a livable wage, and there shouldn't be income taxes taken out of your paycheck. To me, income taxes makes you feel like you are being punished for working. I know the government says that your employer should pay you a lot more because of equity, but you don't have the responsibility of paying for the overhead expenses. If the government really wants to prove that they care, they should stop punishing people and businesses with high taxes and with unnecessary regulations.

Next, people complain about wage inequality between men, women, and minorities. Personally, I believe that instead of paying everyone the same, people should be paid by work performance, knowledge, and dependability. I have worked with people who just want to socialize more than work. It doesn't seem fair that they make the same amount of money as I did when I worked harder and did a better job. People should be paid according to their ability to do the best job, their experience, and their attitude toward providing their employer with the best job performance that will help the business thrive. After all, without a job, you don't have a fair self-sufficient way of paying your bills or feeding your family. Maybe that's why many today want to support socialism, but they don't really understand what will be the payback for free stuff. Just some thoughts.

Another workplace complaint for minorities and women is that there are more white men getting better wages and job positions.

This might be true to some extent, but one needs to look at why this might be the case. Is it possible that you don't have the same responsibilities or experience? Maybe they are given more money because they asked for more wages? Also, just because of the fact that most of this country's population are Caucasian would affirm that there will probably be more whites who are hired. Also, the work values and work ethics might be the reason that you see this disparity. Again, I encourage people to do their best and not look at what someone else gets or doesn't get. If you aren't happy with your job, wouldn't it be better to just move on and get a better-paying job or start your own business? In the meantime, it might even be good to think about how you can become a better person.

Government Oversight or Government Control

Even though I do not like government oversight because government can be very intrusive and/or controlling, they are a necessary evil. But this evil needs to be monitored by the people who elected them. There needs to be some accountability and random auditing by a private organization, or maybe a group of bipartisan taxpayers in order to keep the politicians and government agencies honest. After all, each year, the IRS expects tax laws to be followed. Even the IRS occasionally decides that they will audit a person's financial records just to make sure that they have filed their taxes properly. This might seem somewhat of an inconvenience, but it usually helps deter fraud and keep the taxpayer honest. Therefore, it doesn't seem unreasonable for government agencies to meet the same standards that the American citizens have to meet.

Next, it seems that a lot of the government agencies are unnecessary and/or could be combined with another sector of the government. Example: if the IRS was to be combined with the labor department. Combining agencies could also help save time and make it easier to cross check for fraud. It might even be a better way to change the tax code in order to use a flat fair tax across all divisions of government. A fair flat tax would be beneficial to all taxpayers, and the criteria for all people including the very rich would also be fair. Of course, some people believe that the top 10 percent should pay more because they are so rich. Well, a flat fair tax would do just that. If a flat fair federal tax of 5 percent and a flat fair tax for state were 5 percent for everyone, then every person, including the millionaires and billionaires, would be paying their share of taxes. Although it sounds like I want the rich to pay more, it actually would still allow for most business expenses. The fair tax would be even across the board for all taxpayers. Of course, even though a person who makes $12,000 a year would pay a lot less than a billionaire, they would still be paying their share.

Of course, the government shouldn't be allowed to overtax someone by having taxes such as a death tax. Once a person has paid their taxes on their property or money earned while living, then their children shouldn't have to be taxed for what they inherit. If I remember right, one of the reasons for the Revolutionary War was because of taxation upon taxation. When a government continually comes up with new ways to get money from the citizens through taxes, it becomes a burden, and it seems like you're being punished for working. The taxpayers should be able to call for a special election to block any unnecessary use or abuse of taxpayers and tax dollars. It might even be necessary to vote for people who don't believe that they should tax people, or spend taxes for whatever they decide just because they are powerful and think no one can stop them. Hopefully, there are still more people in America who would be fair-minded, and not all politicians are greedy or self-serving. Also, if voters would vote for politicians who would spend our tax dollars better instead of taxing working people to death. Another term for the government overtaxing people is that overtaxing is just away to legally rob you blind and still tell you they care.

Another area of government is the way that tax dollars are spent. Usually, federal tax expenditures are more wasteful than state or local, but there is plenty of waste and unnecessary spending that benefits the politicians or others instead of the American taxpayers. One such example is politicians give a lot of money to foreign countries, or supply hostile people with military equipment. Why? Who provided this type of help when this country was being formed? No one! You see, people eventually can help themselves if they get tired of their situation. I'm not saying that we shouldn't help people become more self-sufficient, but if they have internal conflicts, and they are a corrupt place, let them figure it out themselves. It makes no sense to rebuild countries after the war ends either. Just look how Europe treats us, and we saved their butts. They don't seem to appreciate our help and don't seem to understand what their lives would have been like if Americans hadn't stepped up to help. It seems ridiculous that people think we should look at the example of any other country because our country outshines them all, and we didn't need them to fight our battles. If you like other countries better than the United States, more power to you, but you need to put actions behind your words; otherwise, to me, you're not a credible person. Just some thoughts.

Another way that government wastes taxpayer's money is supporting projects that don't make sense. For example: studying why chimps throw their feces. Well, it doesn't take much thought or money to reason why they do this behavior. I believe they do this behavior because, just like other animals, they are marking their territory to let other creatures know that this territory is occupied. Another reason might also be that they don't want the crap close to them, or maybe they are letting others know what they think of them. It could even be giving the other chimps the middle figure gesture, or it helps them to relieve stress. Anyway, if someone needs to know this information, let them ask for donations, or get some of these rich politicians to help. Maybe they could align with a private business or person who think that studying chimps throwing its crap is important. Anyway, how does studying chimps throwing their crap help us become better people or cure diseases? Again, if some people think that learning why chimps throw their feces is important, then maybe a private company or person might be interested in learning more about this behavior, but don't waste taxpayer's money. Hopefully, politicians will learn and understand how to spend tax dollars on necessary projects that make life easier for the people of this country. Maybe the government might study why politicians don't seem to get their work done for the people that they are supposed to be serving. If politicians did this, they probably could lower the national debt within ten years. We can only hope and pray that more politicians will start spending and making better decisions with taxpayer's dollars.

Last, politicians make too much money for what they do and for the number of hours that they actually work. This reminds me of when the congress decides to vote on cost of living pay raises the results will always be self-serving. This is the perfect example and meaning of a self-serving politicians. They like giving themselves pay raises, but they have a problem with people getting full retirement payments. I paid into two different retirement plans, and I'm not allowed to get both retirements in full. I'm not sure why or how one should affect the other, but I'm sure that the government will benefit from my loss. It seems unfair for me that some people might be lucky to get only a lower four-figure income from their retirement. I understand that congress decided to take money from people's retirement in the eighties or nineties in the last century. When a person works hard, they should not have the government deciding to take part of either retirement. People work hard to save for their retirement, and politicians who become millionaires after they have been in congress should not get to tell taxpayers anything about their retirement. Maybe the taxpayers should start telling these politicians how much they are allowed to make while in congress. I'm not sure how one fights the powerful people in government. What I am sure about is that the people in government will probably not be held to account if the taxpayers don't insist or change the current way that government is allowed to continue being self-serving wasteful managers of taxpayer's dollars. After all, taxpayers have to be accountable to the government for paying taxes. Just some thoughts.

Government: Functional or Dysfunctional

Government is made up of three co-equal branches. Each with a purpose and specific parameters that are supposed to keep the government functional. The executive branch's responsibilities, just to name a few, are keeping Americans safe, securing the borders, and making sure that people have an economy that creates a prosperous environment. The economic environment in which all citizens have a chance to work and make a living that takes care of their families. Of course, there are other duties of the executive branch, but these areas are the most important. The legislative branch is supposed to write various laws and statutes that help maintain the intended parameters specific to that law. These laws are supposed to reflect and should be based on the constitution of the United States. Therefore, laws should provide all people with guidelines on how they should conduct themselves and how they benefit within a pluralistic society. The judicial branch has the job of interpreting these laws or bills. In a perfect world, these three branches of government would work as intended, but there is one problem: people who have this much power tend to only apply rules as they see fit, and these rules are applied to benefit them. Of course, it's human nature to do this but that doesn't mean that it's right, legal, lawful, or even a logical thing to do. I don't believe that any person is going to do everything perfectly, but they should have to be fair and held accountable when they don't follow the rules that they expect from others. I've learned over the years that people are people, and therefore, they don't always see or do the right thing. That's why it's necessary to experience the consequences of one's actions. This usually has a deterrent effect for the person who abuses the law and other people who see the results of these bad decisions will hopefully think twice before committing the same error.

Government agencies want you to be dependent on them especially the socialists and progressive politicians. This isn't just a conspiracy thinking, it's a way to control the masses. Just stop and think about what I'm saying because socialism is designed to take away your freedom, but it also is a way the powerful can hinder you from doing what's best for yourself and your loved ones. Remember, there is no free cheese in the mousetrap. Socialism is just away that gives the government more control and power. People need to be careful when they vote because most elected officials, once they get elected, rarely follow through with their promises, and some are there until the day they die. In reality, politicians or government always get more than they give. If you think the rich has treated you badly, just wait and see how a socialist government treats its citizens. It's sad, but most people don't learn from others' mistakes. Politicians tell you that you don't need to worry about being treated badly by the rich anymore because they are going to be the modern-day Robin Hoods who take from the rich and give to the poor. But in reality, this is actually just another way for them to become more powerful. Socialism is just a way that keeps the people from having enough power to live independent from the government. Free never means it's free. There is always something they get in return, and there is something you will always lose. Just some thoughts.

If you still believe that the government isn't controlling, then just look at the social programs that are already in place such as Medicaid or Medicare. If you get this insurance, then powers to be can tell you whether they think a procedure is necessary. That's just one example. Another example is what might happen in the future when the government takes away the right to say no to what they deem necessary. Maybe if you don't want to get a certain vaccine for yourself or your children, then they might take some of the free money back or maybe even take your children or lock you up. Remember, congress passes the laws, and they have the right to do whatever they think if you don't comply. Just look at what they are doing to President Trump. Congress has every right not to like Trump, but they want to destroy him because he doesn't live by the unspoken rules of the embedded swamp. It might seem far-fetched, or isn't the best example, but can you see there is a good chance that you may not even have a say in your health care options. If that doesn't help you in understanding why free isn't free, then here's another scenario. Let's look at free health care when the government gets to have access to all your medical and other private information. What are the possibilities that someone who is in power might use your information to deny you services based on your religion, ethnicity, age, or gender, or using this information for ways that may harm you? Example: what if someone around the world needs a donor to continue living? Is it possible that your medical records could be sold for illegal or unethical purposes? I believe if all your medical records are available for these rich powerful politicians, then it's not difficult to believe that they could find someone who is willing to pay the right price. Therefore, it isn't difficult to think that you could be forced to donate your body parts, or worse, they would eliminate you.

Another aspect of government-controlled health care is if they think it's not cost effective, then they may not even allow you to receive a lifesaving procedure due to your age, race, etc. There are so many things that you might not like if you decide to allow the government to be in control of your health care. It's just too risky given that people can be self-serving and evil. This is true, especially when money and power is involved. Just think. Women in New York can now get an abortion even up until the due date or during labor. Doctors may be mandated to let the baby die even if there is a good chance that they could live. If the government can convince people that there is no harm in killing a little precious baby, then what do you think they can do if they want to justify killing anyone else? It sounds like I'm just a paranoid person, and this would never happen, but there has been past abuses of using certain group for experimental studies on syphilis. Here's another thought. Ask yourself why some people in our government wants people to believe that the Jewish people never faced such terrible things during the holocaust and German death camps. Also, you might want to think about how and why Hitler was able to get so many people to do his dirty work.

Finally, as for me, I believe that even though capitalism isn't perfect, it might be better to go the capitalist's way and work for your money. The fact is nothing is perfect, but capitalism is the closest government that provides people away to improve their lives, to live a safer life, and to be able make decisions that will make you happy. As long as we are a free nation, you will be able to live free, and you will be able to make most of the decision that are best for you and your family. Less government and being able to live independent from the government is a good thing for everyone. After all, even though our way of government isn't perfect, there have been many people who have benefited from capitalism and the constitution construct. Just some thoughts.

Grinch on Steroids

Christmas is a time of celebration. It's a time that people think of others and enjoy giving. It's a time for people who are Christians to honor their savior's birth. It's a time that children enjoy meeting and getting gifts from Santa Claus. Why then are some people so miserable that they can't let others enjoy themselves? What reason do people have in thinking it's okay to impose their own ideology into other people's lives? Why do people want to make others as miserable as themselves? Sure, Christmas is a time for Christians to celebrate the birth of Christ, but it also is a time for families and friends to show their love and generosity to others. Christmas is truly a gift to one's children because parents need a real-life example to help their children and others how to care and how giving to others is important. I just have a hard time understanding why some people want to destroy others' beliefs and happiness. The only thoughts that I can come up with are that these people are so miserable, they can't stand that others aren't miserable. Or maybe people who want to crash Christmas for everyone else just have a hard time holding on to their own beliefs, and they need to get rid of any and all things that might give them enough doubts to question their own reasoning.

Christmas is one of the best times I can remember from my childhood. Even though we were poor and didn't get a lot of material things as presents, we still enjoyed Christmas. Even my dad, who was an atheist, still enjoyed Christmas. My dad made sure we always had a tree by getting permission from our neighbors to cut down a tree from their property. Then my brother and I enjoyed making and creating our own decorations. Even though my dad was an atheist, he didn't condemn the holiday, nor did he keep us from going to church and learning about Christ. We were always expected to think for ourselves, and he didn't try to keep us from learning other views that may or may not have contradicted his views.

What I enjoy most about the Christmas season is how it brings people together through the enjoyment of music, festivities, feelings of hope, and a general feeling of goodwill. You would think that people would encourage more holidays that are so uplifting. Also, most people seem to share with others they know and some even share with people with whom they have no association. Yet they gladly give to others. Isn't that a good thing? To me, as a child, Christmas gave me a sense of hope and enjoyment, and I still, after many years, get the same sense of hope and enjoyment during Christmas. Personally, I don't understand people who hate this time of year, and it's also hard to understand how anyone can feel depressed.

To me, Christmas is a positive thing for our society. Yet there are people who have a problem with Christmas, which is okay for them, but why do they want to ban it for the rest of us just because they don't believe in God? So you can imagine how hard it is for me to listen to a group of atheist malcontents who want a monolithic society that reflexes their miserable thinking. It's my opinion that it's not because they don't believe in God but that Christmas triggers questions in their mind that causes them to look at the possibilities that there might be a God. I say this because my father was an atheist, yet he wasn't threatened by our celebrating the Christmas holidays. You see, he allowed us kids to develop our own thinking and encouraged us to think independently from our friend instead of just following what everyone else thought or believed. My dad was a true atheist because he never once considered that Christmas could be anything but fun for children. What's always amazing to me is that others can't seem to respect other people's rights to celebrate what they want to celebrate. I don't disrespect the rights of people to choose atheism as their bases for looking at life. How would atheists like someone trying to band them from something they enjoy? Maybe this might help them understand that others have the right to believe in Christmas. Why is Christmas such an issue when there are still more people in America are Christians, and this holiday is very important for Christians to celebrate in honor of their beliefs?

Why do people like atheists and others who have doubts about God think that they are freethinkers when they contradict themselves? Their thinking and attitudes show that they are anything but freethinkers. Maybe these freethinkers never heard the saying, "Live and let live." Instead of seeing Christmas as a problem, why don't they just find their own way of celebrating that there is no God? Please, just leave the rest of us alone and stop being so controlling. Also, you need to get a life and let others believe and celebrate what they chose, and I will continue to leave them to their way of thinking. Believe me, I could talk all day about why I believe in God the Father, his Son, and the Holy Spirit. Do I have any challengers? If you truly choose to deny that God doesn't exist, then please don't be threatened by my explanation of what I have outlined in this opinion. Instead of condemning Christians, maybe you should do positive things like donating to a monolithic groups that need to feel miserable in order to feel relevant.

Last, I'm so thankful that my parents taught us to think independently. It has helped me to be open-minded and not threatened by others' views. Maybe instead of feeling threatened by a holiday, maybe you could just look at people like myself as if you pity me for my misguided, uninformed, or uneducated lack of understanding. Seeing and thinking that others just don't have the ability to reason is how I view people who think like atheists, or others who can't live or let live. Oh, by the way, I have a college degree plus it only helps reinforce my religious beliefs. I still cannot understand why my dad was an atheist because he was a very intelligent man. Personally, I don't have the time or desire to tell others how they should live their lives. Treat others as you want to be treated. It will be a great Christmas gift to yourself and others. Merry Christmas and get a life. Just some thoughts.

Humans versus Animals

One of the first papers that I decided to write about in college was *What Makes Us Humans*. Of course, I've always believed there are some significant differences between humans and animals. I really didn't think much about human behavior as a child but became more interested in understanding the differences between humans and animals while I was working toward a psychology degree. The reason I decided to write a paper about these differences was due to a comment that another church member said about my daughter. My daughter looked perfectly normal when she was born. She never did develop the ability to speak or walk without falling. When this older woman said that I should just put her with her own kind, it just felt like she had stepped on my heart. It never occurred to me that my daughter needed to be put with strangers just because she couldn't walk or talk. In fact, I couldn't fully understand at first what this lady meant by "put her with her own kind." She was my beautiful daughter, and I would never in my worst day abandon my child. I love my daughter and think of her as a human being with feelings. It did concern me that there was a big possibility that she might never be able to live an independent life as an adult. This lady's comment wasn't helpful for me or my daughter. Another reason for my interest was to educate ignorant people about others who are born with challenges doesn't mean that they should be put somewhere else. Of course, because she was elderly, I didn't tell her to mind her own business. I kept thinking why did she think that my daughter isn't as human as the rest of us. Of course, this hurt me deeply, and I just couldn't understand how anyone could make such a cruel comment. Also, it just added to my fear that my daughter would always be rejected by others just because she was different. It took me a long time to accept that she would never talk, walk, or be able to live as an independent adult. I never felt she wasn't human or needed to be put with "her own kind" but because I wanted to prove to that lady that my daughter was just like me and was already with her own kind.

Understanding the difference between humans and animals was going to help me make a good argument that would help others see that being human isn't because you are perfect, but rather, you are human because you have the ability to think and care about others. Being human shouldn't be measured by your IQ, but rather, by your ability to care about others. She was a human because she was able to feel emotions. My daughter is kind to others and brightens my day with her smile that gives me a sense that she might even be more human than the rest of so-called people.

To begin my study of what the differences were that separated us from animals, I decided to ask one of my professors what he believed was the difference between humans and other animals. He commented that the only thing that he could think of was that humans can communicate through written words. This made sense to me, but didn't animals have their own way of writing messages to others around them? After all, as a child, I would read a lot about various species to learn more about their behavior and other interesting details that were specific to that species. I was also fortunate to live in the mountains where you can see firsthand about wild animals, and of course, I could observe my cats' and dogs' behaviors. At the time, I thought that my animals weren't much different when it came to needing to be shown kindness and other behaviors that seemed to resemble people's behaviors. From these similarities between various body tissues and physical structures of some animals helps scientists understand various physiological process and other things that can help researchers learn and understand ways to help in medicine and other areas of human life. These researchers can use various studies of animals to help scientists make an educated reasonable inference that benefits humans and animals in general. Personally, it's my belief that we can learn a lot about life and survival when we study animals and their habitats. Native Americans used what they learned from observing animal behavior to help them survive and even predict environmental events such as weather.

What I believe is the biggest difference between animals and humans has to do with the structure of the brain and our ability to develop a conscience that helps us think about how we treat others. Also, it's interesting to try and understand why others' lack of a conscience allow us to become evil. Due to my observations and studies about both animals and humans, I've concluded that animals can demonstrate signs of empathy, but they don't seem to have the ability to kill out of hate. I have observed one of my dogs act like they had some form of a conscience and seemed to exhibit being ashamed of their misdeeds. Another difference that humans have is the ability (as we get into our teen years) to use abstract ideas to solve complex problems. Of course, since I believe in creation, we are told, and I have read, that God created us in his own image. I do believe this to be true. What it means to be made in God's image to me means that humans have the ability to care, think about the future, understand consequences, empathize (my dog has that ability), understand and predict behavior, and experience a long range of emotions. Of course, all humans can learn or choose to do good or evil. Animals kill out of hunger, or when they feel threatened. Humans can kill out of hate, or kill just because they decided someone or something doesn't deserve to live. Also, humans kill for survival reasons and can kill to protect themselves. In other words, animals don't want to destroy. They just want to live for today. Animals also don't seem to hold grudges like humans can.

One last comment about humans versus animals. I believe that humans can learn by example to understand others. They also can learn to show and feel empathy for others, care for others, and respect others. Humans can learn concepts such as treat others like you want to be treated. Animals can demonstrate love toward other creatures and learn various behaviors with or without training, but they cannot reason or be judged evil just because they do something that we deem as evil. What I do believe is that people and animals can both learn good or bad behavior. Therefore, it's important to raise all children and pets in an environment that is safe, loving, caring, thoughtful, consistent, and drug free. Also, it's important to encourage children to make good choices and provide them with learning experience that includes sports, hobbies, music, or art, and don't forget to encourage healthy habits. I believe that anyone can learn and contribute to society regardless of any disability. Everyone is important and deserves respect. One of the most important observation I know to be true about people is the ability people have to change their behavior. Last, anyone can rise above their circumstances if they decide and they can become a better person who is capable of giving and caring about themselves and others.

Immigration Documented versus Undocumented

This subject is one that I am conflicted with and hesitate to give an opinion. This is because I think more with my heart, and I have a hard time making tough decisions. Immigration has always been part of Americans' success stories, and no one can make a good argument that can convince me otherwise, but folks, we need to look at what immigration really means.

In the past, in order to come and stay in America, you needed to prove who you were, what were your intentions for wanting to become a citizen, were you disease-free, and you needed to be self-sufficient and contribute positive to the current society. Many of us have ancestors that came to America from another country. Our ancestors came to America so that they could have a better life that only America could give them. They didn't believe that they had every right to come here regardless of their intentions, but they understood that to come to America, you needed to learn the language and that they needed to contribute and become integrated socially into the ideas of American success and greatness. The reason for this criteria was to make sure that they were able to fit into a free society and become a contributing member that would get along with others. In return, they would be provided all that it means to be an American citizen. Also, they would be able to live an independent life of freedom with the possibility of improving their living conditions. There was no question that they had to take care of themselves and their families.

Today, immigration from most countries still respect the process of becoming a citizen, but there are others who believe that they don't have to play by the same rules. Therefore, if you can get across the border, or can find a way to claim asylum, then you have every right to be in America, and you can benefit from taxpayers with no questions asked. Also, if you question their reasoning, you're considered a hateful and cruel bigot. What kind of thinking is this? I don't, nor would I expect another country to just allow me to show up and not be expected to follow the rules of that country. But, of course, I'm an American through and through and wouldn't think of living in a different country. I also realize how fortunate I am because of the fact I was born and raised in America. I also understand that most people just want a better life, and they believe that coming to America will provide hope for them and their families. But in order for America to remain free and great, people need to immigrate lawfully, learn the language, and leave their country's way of thinking behind them.

Personally, if I could protect all children from evil and poverty, I would, but even Jesus told his disciples that there will always be poverty. Maybe for the folks who don't have the money to become a citizen legally, they could find some way of raising the money, or find someone to sponsor them so that they can become a legalized citizens. I've known some very good people who migrated from Mexico and think they are overall great people. They have contributed a lot as a citizen, and they are usually very humble people who like America. It's hard for me to say this, but no country can just allow everyone to come in the country without them being screened and without them being able to take care of their own family. Just some thoughts.

Last, asylum seekers or anyone else should not automatically have every right afforded to people who were born and raised in this country. There should be a certain amount of years that they can prove themselves as people who will contribute and love our country. They should prove that they love this country enough to be building it up, not trying to make it like their mother country. It's my opinion that anyone who gets asylum in America and then slams our way of life, then they should be required to go back to the country they came from, or go to another country that is more to their liking. Although I'm not sure what other country who would be willing to take such an ungrateful hate fueling individual who don't deserve to be in America. Another group of people who shouldn't be allowed to stay are the ones that were born here but think that they live in the worst country. Well, my thoughts are, *Why do they stay?* I'm sure that Russia would be happy to welcome them into their great country. Sure, this country has its problems, but America provides more positive chances than not, and no other country can compare to the blessings that God has provided America. May God continue to bless America. Just some thoughts.

Israel and America's Friendship

I believe that America is the most blessed nation on this planet because we are friends of Israel, and we as Christians are required to be allies with Israel. I believe that this friendship with Israel is encouraged within the context of scriptures, and God's blessings are contingent to America remaining a blessed nation. Since we are still overall a blessed Christian nation that seeks guidance from the Holy Bible, it is crucial to Americans' well-being. People, we need to realize that being friends with Israel may be the only reason God is still blessing this country. It is very sad that we can't say anymore that most of America still lives to honor God the Father, Jesus, his Son, and the Holy Spirit. Instead, we have become a nation that wants to change our ideals into what people believe is a compassionate nation. Of course, being compassionate is a good thing, but what isn't a good thing is being careless with who we allow into this country, or how we allow others to change the fabric of America, and this includes trying to make people more politically correct.

This country was built on Christian values, and these values use to be reverenced and followed by more people than not. In today's society, having the Ten Commandments in a courthouse is illegal, and people blame the tenants of the Bible for all the ills of society. Instead of blaming others or God for America's problems, people need to self-reflect on how they can be a better person and contribute to keeping this a nation a safe and prosperous haven. A haven that is thankful to a God that provides so much for the health and well-being of America's people. I believe that the reason God blesses us with so much is because there are still people who recognize that hard work and honoring God is the way to receiving many blessings. I once heard a professor talk about a Russian dignitary who stood in the bread isle in a city market grocery mart. He said the Russian was awestruck on how much bread was in just one isle because food is quite often scarce in his country. America, how great God's grace is to thee. Also, how great that men and women of faith were the ones who struggled against great odds along with their faith to develop this country into a safe prosperous nation. Again, Israel being an ally is an important component for our nation, and it's important for us to continue being a friend of Israel. It is my hope that God will continue to have mercy on the people of this great nation because of our strong alliance with Israel. Just some thoughts.

Me Too or Me Money

Where does one begin to understand the motives of people except from observations, motivations, evidence, and their own personal experience? I'm sure that every situation isn't going to have the same conclusions, but one can figure out overall what might be happening in most cases. One of the current social dilemma that I will be commenting on is this Me Too movement. As a woman, I can relate to what is being reported by other women. But I'm convinced that just because a woman is claiming that she is being sexually harassed or raped on or off the job doesn't mean it should automatically be believed. This is especially true if it's been more than a year before she decides to take action against the person. After a year, there may be a problem convincing people of the validity of your complaint in question.

What women should do after they have truly been a victim is never blame themselves but be honest with themselves so that they aren't just trying to make trouble for the guy. Example: if you decide to go to a party, and you know that there is going to be alcohol and possibly other drugs, then you might not want to put yourself in this situation. People who go to these type of parties should expect there will be bad behaviors. If you choose to still go, then you have a couple of safety rules that you might want to remember. Make sure you have friends who are with you or friends that will be attending the party. Next, don't go up to a bedroom or other places where you are alone with any guy. It might help make it clear to a guy, because you don't want to give mixed messages to a guy, especially if you don't know the person. I disagree that it's just up to the guy to stop, but women also need to take responsibility in these type of situations. If women are going to consider themselves strong capable women, then they need to make better decisions instead of putting themselves into a situation that makes it easy for them to be a victim who can't take care of themselves. But, of course, if a guy forces, or a guy drugs, or if you are unconscious, then it truly is sexual assault. I'm not a guy, so I'm not sure why some guys like to have sex with women who are not available to participate, but it does happen.

I just think that women are capable of avoiding certain situations, but I know some people think that they shouldn't need to be afraid or avoid anything. My comment to them is that I agree to a certain point. It would be nice if I could just leave my door unlocked and never have anything stolen from me. Have you ever heard that an ounce of prevention is worth a pound of cure? But if they truly believe that they are a victim, they should determine what action they need to take against the person who has committed the crime within a reasonable amount of time.

I believe that most women have experienced unwanted harassment from others, whether it's sexual in nature, or just harassment in general. It is clear to me that when dealing with men or women, one needs to communicate clearly to them the first two times that the unwanted behavior occurs. Be sure to make it clear to a person that you don't want them harassing you. Also, a person needs to be firm about how they feel and let them know that you will press charges if they continue. As for communicating to the person who is harassing you, again, it is important that you make sure that they understand that their behavior is not welcome. It's hard to believe in today's societal norms, or even forty years ago, that women don't know how to communicate to others what they don't like. My suggestion is if someone you don't want any association and they ignore you, then do what I do. I give a person no more than two warnings, then if they don't get the hint and continue an unwanted behavior, I let them know that I will press harassment charges against them if they try bothering me the third time. The secret to getting them to leave you alone is follow through with your warnings.

Of course, rape is more serious and needs to be dealt with immediately. If you don't want to go directly to the police, then find a family member, friend, clergy, or someone else who you can trust and let them know right away. The best thing to do is go directly to a medical facility so that they can preserve all evidence. One concern I have though is what people now considers rape. Again, if two people are out partying and end up having sex, then it may be questionable whether it's rape. If you are drinking, and the guy continues unwanted moves, maybe you need to push them away and let them know firmly that you're not interested in having sex. You don't want to say one thing and then continue letting or participating in any form of intimate behavior. If you do, it's my opinion that you are giving mixed messages that contributes to the guy's behavior. I can't emphasize this enough: be sure you let the guy know that you will not tolerate his behavior, even if you need to find someone else to take you home.

If a rape does occur, then the victim will usually have evidence like some serious bruising from a confrontation, or trying to get away. When there is no physical evidence, witness, or some other proof, then how can rape be proven? When a person is being accused of such a serious crime, one that can ruin their life, then it seems fair that it be investigated thoroughly. Why should women always be believed and not the man? No one wants a woman to be treated unfairly, but no one should want a guy who didn't rape them to be labeled as a sex offender either. I make this difference between forcible and so-called date rape because I have known of women who use sex to get back at a guy, or they use sex to control them, or they have regrets and don't want to be blamed for engaging in sexual acts for whatever reason.

The problem I see with this Me Too movement is that because women wait for so long to report the incident that one has to wonder why they waited so long. I understand that some of these women might be reluctant to come forward right away, but why do women wait until the man becomes rich and famous? Some have even been public figures, or they are running, or they were picked for a justice of the Supreme Court. It just seems to be convenient when a woman complains, and they finally come forward when the man is wanting to be a judge or a president. After all, these men have been public figures for a long time. When women claim that they were afraid but then all of a sudden realized after thirty-five years that they have developed more confidence, then they definitely shouldn't be believed. Especially if they are college professors who are feminists. Another comment I want to say about another woman who tried to smear Judge Kavanagh's credibility during his confirmation hearing was the creepy porn lawyer's client. She was the one who said that she witnessed Kavanagh, when he was a teen, partaking into lining up with other boys to force sex onto their victims. My questions is why did she keep going back? Why didn't she report it to the police or someone else? After all, she was over twenty-one and possibly could get into trouble for not reporting a crime? I'm a firm believer that people who lie to cause others problems should be held accountable for their actions and not just verbally reprimanded. Last, anyone who goes to powerful men's apartments for their interview need to stop being naive. There is no job on Earth that would make me sleep with a creep, and I would not go to a place that puts me alone with a creep. Again, these women should have told someone else at the time it occurred. My main concern is that when rape or sexual assault gets watered down, then it's easy to accuse just about every guy of being a sexual predator. It's been my experience as a woman that most men will make comments, or they will make a pass on a date as a way of getting the woman to have sex with them. Therefore, the woman should stop being a victim and communicate clearly what you will not agree with or what you will allow.

One last comment is that I believe that parents should encourage their children to be assertive if necessary in a relationship. Also, I believe that parents should teach children by example how to interact with the opposite sex. If a mother or father is abusive, or makes sex an issue, then there will most likely be fertile ground for problems with how their children interact with the opposite sex. Parents teach a lot of behaviors by role modeling healthy communication. I'm not saying that children need to learn about how Mom and Dad interact sexually. What I'm saying is that children need to learn how to interact with others in a healthy way. Also, let both your sons and daughters know that they are loved and important so that they don't look for love and acceptance in all the wrong places. I understand that even the most loving parents can't always be responsible for their teen or adult children's behavior. This is especially true in today's social atmosphere where anything is normal, accepted, and drug use is more acceptable. Just some thoughts.

My Philosophy

There are some things that a person believes or lives by that are not negotiable. My foundation of what I believe about spiritual matters and what I believe about people are not necessarily the same. I'm a Christian and believe in the trinity (the Father, the Son, and the Holy Spirit), but it's not my job to judge others souls. There are other spiritual beliefs that I live by, and they probably have roots in my Native American ancestry. Some of which are things like respecting and learning from nature and animal behavior. I don't believe that we should kill just to be killing, but rather, to kill what's necessary for food that sustains life and keeps a person healthy. Even though I don't believe we should kill others, I do believe in self-defense.

It's my belief that people are made in the image of God, therefore, we should show respect to others. Also, because God created all things, I believe that we should be careful on how we use Earth's resources, and we should respect all living things. This doesn't mean that I should trust all people because they are all good, nor should I try to change things because I believe they are evil. Quite to the contrary, I believe that people can be evil or good, and their behaviors toward others can clearly demonstrate that to be true. I also believe people have the capacity to change and make decisions that have good or bad consequences.

Some of my core beliefs are based on the New Testament, such as treat others like you want to be treated, don't repay evil with evil, be positive about life (I have to work on this), treat everyone with kindness but don't expect them to reciprocate, and I don't think that this is what makes them a good or an evil person. I also believe that I can't judge others' soul, but rather, God is the one that judges all our hearts from which behavior is developed. Because I am human, I am not perfect and have bad days when I can be rude. When I am rude, I usually try to apologize because I believe it's me with the problem, not the person I'm directing my unhappiness toward. I apply this rule to others who are rude by understanding that they may just be having a bad day.

I believe that children are people, too, and deserve to be treated with the understanding that they are learning and can make mistakes. To me, children need to be protected and guided by parents who are emotionally attached to them. I don't believe that a child should be used or abused, but parents should be consistent with how they discipline. Also, I believe that physical punishment shouldn't be viewed as abusive just because some person who has power say it's abusive. It's my belief that a parent is more abusive by letting children do whatever they want to do, and they are left without someone teaching them how to make better decisions. I do believe though that it couldn't hurt for all people to take courses in child development before becoming a parent. This is important because developmental levels do make a difference in a child's understanding and behavior. That's why you need to show children patience and understanding first and punishment for the last resort. One of the most important part of raising children is to communicate to them how their behavior affects others. I believe a mom and a dad are very important for children to learn how to socially behave toward males and females. Also, behaviors and attitudes can be learned by what children observe in their environment. For people that think that children don't see their attitudes about others and how they respond to life's various challenges, you are sadly mistaken. On the other hand, children can learn many good behaviors from observing others. I didn't realize this until my children would repeat being kind and considerate to others, and I remember a time that they repeated something I didn't necessarily want everyone to know. It can get embarrassing.

I also believe it's important to give a child a consistent predictable environment from which they will develop a strong foundation for times that aren't predictable. Of course, a child needs also to learn from natural consequences in order for them to develop the tools and confidence that are necessary in dealing with problems throughout their lives. These tools will help them recognize they are valuable and have the confidence to solve problems. The things that children learn about problem-solving as children can be connected, not only to natural consequences but also to learning math. I believe that is especially true when doing word math problems. Just learning fractions while learning to follow a recipe is another way to teach solving problems. School isn't the only way children learn their basics in math and other subjects.

I also believe that mental illness has its roots in when a person's fears, guilt, or shame is overblown and when they don't learn to manage their anger. Anyone can become mentally ill if they don't have the necessary tools to deal with their emotions in a healthy manner. This is why parents should let their children play sports, or get them involved in other programs like art and music. When children participate in sports, or other competitive interactions, they can learn how to share and learn to deal with disappointments in life that are destined to happen to all people. If a child grows up without learning that life can have consequences beyond our control, then they will turn to unhealthy ways of dealing with their emotional reactions to disappointments and losses. Another benefit of competitions is that children learn to interact with a team and learn to plan and figure out the possibilities of ways to win. What I believe is one of the most important lessons for children when they are involved in any healthy activity is that they experience learning the sense of well-being by focusing on the here and now.

I do believe that emotions are a necessary part of having a good mental health, and I don't think that because a person shows anger that society should equate that as being mean or crazy. Anger can be good as long as it doesn't become a way of hurting or harming self or others. My belief is that when people don't express anger in a healthy way, then they will express it in unhealthy dangerous ways, or maybe they become bitter angry people who will have health problems. Also, people who hold onto anger can develop unhealthy thinking, which leads to behavior of people verbally lashing out and possibly physically hurting or even killing someone else. Unresolved anger and other emotional issue have been linked to cancer. Last, people need to give other people respect and understanding, not because they like them necessarily but because you don't know what they are capable of, or what they are going through. Like someone once said, "To err is human. To forgive, divine." Just some thoughts.

President Trump

President Trump is the forty-fifth President of the United States of America. It seems that people either love him or hate him. I do believe though that most people find him unique and different from any other person who ran and won the honor of being America's leader and America's world representative. It is refreshing to me when he says what he thinks instead of what he thinks people want to hear. This, to me, is a sign of a truly great leader. Do I agree with everything he says? No. But I agree with more of what he says than not. Instead of a global view, he believes in putting Americans first and making sure that the rest of the world pays their fair share. Also, President Trump says what he thinks and actually gets his agenda for America accomplished. Other politicians test what they think is going to get them elected and say it in such a way that it's obvious that they are pandering to someone other than the patriotic taxpayers. People who vote for these pandering politicians don't seem to care whether they keep America safe or not. All they seem to care about is what they hear or maybe how much freebies they may get. Then once these politicians get into office, they either don't do what they said they would do, or they do the opposite. Most politicians think that they can get by with this pandering and that no one will care because most people vote along party lines. They also want to keep their lobbyists happy because their lobbyists' provide big money for their campaigns. This is another reason Trump stood out to the taxpayers because he didn't take lobbyists money and therefore didn't owe them any favors.

What I've noticed about President Trump is that he cares about all people and wants the best for all Americans. He has done more in his first three years than all the rest combined have done in the last fifty years. Also, President Trump has been able to deliver on most of his campaign promises. He was able to do this even during all the hate-filled rhetoric that was used to derail his presidency. It's been disheartening to see how the president gets treated by the so-called elitists and the progressives. If you ask me, I think that people who mistreat people the way they do President Trump should take a good long look at themselves. Also, you can read in the Bible that Jesus pointed out to people that they should first evaluate their own sins before they judge others, and the way we judge others will be the way God judges our sins. To be forgiven, one first needs to forgive others, and I have learned that if I examine my own life, then I am less likely to be critical of others. Also, one of the Ten Commandments states, "Do not bare false witness against others." Another commandment that is very important is to treat others as you want to be treated. Instead of smearing the president, I want the haters to think about the way they treat him, his family, and the American people who voted for him in 2016, and how they might feel if people treated them the way they treat the president.

Next, a lot of people complain about President Trump not standing up to dictators of countries that are known for human rights violations. I believe that President Trump or any president should want to treat them in a way that opens the door for future trade talks. They complain about everything that he does. They tell President Trump how he should handle dealings with foreign enemies but blame him for trying to start wars. It's obvious that nothing President Trump does will ever change or please these hate mongers. Something tells me that his critics would complain about him no matter what the president decided. This is really rich because most of the same politicians that are pointing the finger at him have done the same thing or worse. Also, they didn't think or do anything about these problems until President Trump was in office. It's not because they didn't have enough time because some politicians have been in office so long that being in congress has become a lifestyle. What the problem seems to be is that either they didn't understand the issue enough to solve the problem, or maybe they are just too busy with thinking about getting elected again instead of solving problems for the American people. In fact, most of them didn't even see any problems, or come up with any solutions to these problems until Trump started successfully solving the problems. Congress only thought about these issues after President Trump decided to make changes to various programs. I'm not sure why they think that they needed to take control of how President Trump was changing the status quo, but something tells me that they really don't want the status quo changed. Also, it might help people to understand just how incompetent they are if Trump is successful at solving this country's problems. News flash: people have understood that congress is incompetent for a long time. That's why people voted for a successful businessman. Just maybe if some people in congress would decide to stop hating President Trump, then maybe they could learn ways to better serve the American people. I'm sure that the president would listen to suggestions, but why should he listen to hate-filled, self-serving politicians who daily criticism him and never say anything positive to encourage President Trump? Most people will tend to ignore people who they know are trying to cause them problems. I suggest that the adult in the room needs encouragement, not self-righteous criticism from jealous power mongers.

I'm rather bothered by the way people characterize the president's behavior because he is just himself. Now I know why there are so many phony people who can get away with so much and do themselves and this country a great deal of harm. After the 2018 election reports came out on the news, there was a lot of talk about how many suburban moms voted democrat instead of republican. It was bad enough that the democrats won the house back, but what was even more alarming for me was the reason that suburban moms decided to vote democrat. I couldn't believe that they voted for democrats just because of the way the president talks. I just couldn't believe that they would think more about the way a person talks than what the president has accomplished for the families of this country. My response to the suburban moms or any other taxpaying citizens. What type of leader do you want running this country? A strong leader that keeps you and your children safe? Or do you want a polished politician who doesn't upset your way of thinking? Please, for the sake of other Americans, when you vote, please think about safety. Also, think about how well the economic and the foreign affairs are doing and less about how he presents his message. A voter's first priority should be making sure that we can maintain a free country so that we can freely go about living in a free country. Personally, I could care less if President Trump talks out his butt as long as he works for the betterment of this country.

I want to address the voters who think being phony is better than keeping this country safe and prosperous. I understand that some people have trouble accepting that Trump won in 2016 because I've experienced the same letdown when Obama won the presidency in 2012. The one thing that I can't understand though is the visceral hate you see from a lot of people in government, in the entertainment industry, and worst, in the supposed-to-be-objective media. Where there is hate, there usually is a threat to someone's secrets that they don't want exposed, or it's because it can create a fear that they will lose their power. Some of the Trump haters will make up things about President Trump. Some people say that he's a bigot. Well, I have only seen that he treats minorities like he treats everyone else, and some would say that he treats minorities even better. It's not for me to judge his motives, and it's okay with me that he treats minorities better because he's doing what he thinks will help this part of our society. This is what I think about people who complain about President Trump's treatment of minorities. I don't want to hear it until you denounce Louis Farrakhan and a few other radical people who hate Jewish people and white people, then what you have to say about President Trump might be more credible. Stop being so blind to your own bigotry. Don't let disagreements or hate cloud your judgement.

Last, President Trump won in 2016 because he ran and worked hard to include all people. People from all backgrounds and people who don't like phonies and people who aren't fooled by a smooth-talking, self-serving, and money-loving phony politician. Why do suburban women have such problems with how President Trump talks? Which is better? A phony politician that tells you everything you want to hear? Or a person who has accomplished a lot in keeping America safe and a person who has created or foster an environment that give all people a way to improve their lives? Personally, I could care less if he talks out his butt as long as he makes sure that I can be safe and provides a way for me to prosper through tax cuts. It just boggles my mind that others can't understand that when Obama was president, some of us had to endure the incompetent way he ran this country. We weren't happy with most of his decisions, but we accepted the fact that others felt differently. Just hang in there, folks, and you'll get another president some of these days that will tell you everything you want to hear. Hopefully, for the rest of us, they will continue to keep this country safe and prosperous for our children and grandchildren.

Rights or Special Treatment

If you are born in America or a legalized citizen, you have certain rights that the bill of rights has determined that is God-given and should not be determined by who runs the country or the popular vote of the citizenry. Therefore, I have made a list of which are my rights according to my interpretation. Also, I will compare my rights to what I believe versus your rights when it comes to interacting with me. You might not agree, or even like what I think, but this, again, is how I interpret the bill of rights. Last, if it offends you too much, you might want to think about your motives, or find an island that you can become a king and rule. Again, I will list my rights below and what I think that I don't have a right to do to others. Oh yes, I will tell you that I believe in treating others as I would like to be treated.

I have a right to privacy, but I don't have the right to interfere in another person's life. Unless I have committed a crime against someone's property or person, no one should have the right to interfere with how I live and what I do.

I have a right to pick and choose whom I associate with. No one has the right to force me to like who I don't care to be around. Neither do I have the right to force my ideas on to others.

I have the right to freely move about my city or property without harassment or harm and will act to protect myself regardless of who is trying to harm me. But I don't have the right to go to someone and harass or harm them, even if I don't like them and think they are bigots. Bigots have just as much rights as everyone else. I hate to inform you, but even minorities have bigots among them. There is no culture who is free of bigots.

I have a right to protest, but I do not have the right to tear someone else's property up or threaten people their safety and that includes surrounding their home, car, person, or space. To me, when a person feels threatened, they should be able to defend themselves with any means necessary.

I have a right not to be harassed by government officials, and if they legally can do that, then the citizens should vote for an amendment that keeps people in power from becoming bullies. But I do believe people should respect laws or work toward changing laws of which they disagree. Remember that without laws, there are many bad things that can happen.

I believe that I have the God-given right to pursue life, liberty, and happiness, but I don't believe I have a right to destroy others in the process, nor do I have the right to use or abuse these rights. It's not right to keep someone else from prospering, moving about freely, or take their life so that you think it will advance your rights.

I have a right to believe and worship freely if I'm not torturing or killing another living person or creature. I don't understand atheists, devil worshipping, and people who don't comb their hair, but it's their right. These are the people I have a right to stay away from, but I don't have the right to chase them from my town or harass them.

I have a right to work and use the money as I want, and the government should never have the right to keep taxing whenever they think they need more money. After all, one of the reasons for the Revolutionary War was to keep the people in power from robbing people blind under the guise of needed more money to meet government projects or budget excess. Also, I believe that no one, including the government, should be able to access or track my bank account, unless I owe a debt to them, or the government is helping me with various programs. Also, I don't believe that I have to share my money or property with anyone unless I choose to help others. I believe in paying taxes, but the government has a thirst for money and should be limited to what they think a person should pay. Oh, by the way, I think rich people who have made wise decisions shouldn't have to pay more taxes so others who didn't make good decisions can benefit from their hard work. There is a term for this type of person. They are a leech or a parasite. By the way, I'm not talking about people who truly need help such as people who can't even take care of their own personal needs. It's good that America will take care of the truly needy, not people who just don't want or think that they need to contribute to even their own life. Don't tell me about poor people needing help because compared to how I grew up, even people on government assistance are rich. Compared to other countries, anyone who is blessed to be an American is rich in my way of thinking. Would I like to have more money? Yes, but not if I must take it from someone else who isn't offering it to me or I haven't worked for to earn my way.

I have a right to think for myself and to care for myself, even if someone thinks I'm too old. I do not have the right to tell someone else that they don't know how to take care of themselves. Of course, if some are not able to remember where they are at, or they become a danger to others, then they need help. But that doesn't mean that you have the right to deem someone incompetent just because you don't like them, or they anger you, or because 150 years ago, they did harm to other groups of people. Last, no one has the right to end life without there being no hope for them to recover, such as being brain dead. Of course, this is my personal and religious beliefs. Others think different, but they will have to live and answer for their beliefs.

I have a right to my opinion if I'm not harassing someone or denying them their rights to live a life that they think makes them happy or happier. But I don't have a right to make someone's life miserable just because I don't like them or their opinions.

I have a right to make decisions on how I live, talk with whom I associate, but the government nor anyone else has the right to limit my free speech. Except for when children are involved, I don't have a right to tell others who they should love, even if I believe it to be wrong and I disagree with their thinking. I'm not the one who will judge their souls. My belief is that someday, we all must meet our maker and answer for how we conducted ourselves and how we treated others throughout the process of our life.

Second Amendment: The Constitutional Right

The Second Amendment gives American citizens the right to bear arms, to defend their property, and to defend themselves against a government that becomes tyrannical. The people who fought and won the Revolutionary War knew firsthand that people in power could easily abuse their power if left unchecked. Therefore, in order for people to maintain their freedom against a tyrant, then the government shouldn't be able to become more powerful than the people that they are supposed to serve. This was the common man's way of guaranteeing that their rights wouldn't be easy to take away. Of course, people also used these arms to hunt and protect themselves and their families from various other threats. Threats that they might encounter in life that would require them to defend themselves, their family, or their property. Also, I'm convinced that our forefathers were wanting to make sure that they included all weapons that would be necessary for people to maintain their God-given rights. Of course, I can't fully understand what their reasoning was for the Second Amendment, nor can I fully understand what it was like for them to live under the system of a king as the ruler. Therefore, I can't judge whether their hearts were evil, or how I would have handled life then and because I didn't live or experience what was necessary to do in order to survive during the beginning of this country as we know it today. I think one can conclude that like today, our forefathers understood that evil does exist in some people, and there needs to be a way to fight evil. I believe that our country's forefathers' thinking was when evil goes unchecked, then people needed a way to not become a victim of anyone. Also, the Second Amendment was a way to prevent harm to self and property, and they decided gun ownership was also a way how to prevent government overreach, and also, it was a way to keep government humble.

Then they constructed what the government would look like so that there will be a system of checks and balances. This checks and balances was finally formulated by creating three branches of government. These three branches consists of the executive branch (president) who decides what he believes that most of the people of this country could benefit and what would help maintain a republic that best follows, reflects, and maintains a constitutional free country that serves all people. The legislative branch (house and senate) creates laws that are supposed to serve all the people and maintain some sense of fairness that is constitutionally sound. Finally, the judicial branch is responsible for understanding and interpreting the laws based on the way the constitution was written. All three branches are sworn into office by taking an oath to keep and uphold the constitution precepts. Keeping in mind how our framers laid out a written foundation. This foundation was specifically created so that people could enjoy their God-given rights, and it was a way to help assure people that they would always have a legal base to reason and maintain their freedom. Today, the people who are supposed to be serving the American people have decided to interpret the constitution as a changing document that ends up fitting their agendas. Today's three branches of government consists of some people who have decided that the constitution can be interpreted to mean whatever people want it to mean. This watered-down version of the constitution, as whatever one wants it to mean instead of what is written in the constitution, gives a big avenue for government officials to abuse and take away the people's God-given rights. Therefore, the people are at the mercy of the powers to be instead of the powers to be at the mercy of the people.

Our forefathers understood that without documents like the constitution to guide them that it would be hard to keep and maintain a fairness for all people. Did or does this happen all the time? Probably not. Some would say no because of slavery, but others would say that slavery was just another way to show your social status and was common among people of status. I believe that not all people were cruel to their slaves, and some viewed them more as servants who they needed for doing work. I'm not saying that it was right, but white people are not the only people who have owned slaves. Also, all whites didn't own slaves. Anyway, I don't think that people who founded this country could ever have imagined what would become of this country. After all, our forefathers knew firsthand what it was like to live under a tyrannical government and what it took to be free. I'm just thankful that I didn't live during this time because there was some hard decisions to make just in order to survive.

Getting back to the Second Amendment, I'm convinced that our country's framers couldn't have imagined that some people would or could become so evil with how they used firearms to just kill others. This I can understand because when I was growing up, most people respected life and believed that life was God-given, and therefore, only God had the right to take a life. Everyone that I knew realized that guns were dangerous and care was taken to prevent children from getting access to the firearms. I cannot remember a time that guns were handled carelessly, or used to just kill other living creatures. Even then, I don't believe that anyone could have imagined a life where others would have such a disregard for humans and even a disregard for animals' life. Today, it's a common event to hear about someone going into a place just to kill other people. What's even more alarming is the reaction and inaction you get from politicians. It's the same old mantra. People need to register their guns. How in God's name does that keep people from being evil? Also, it seems to me that most of these killings take place in the states that have stricter gun laws. Another observation is that most gun-related murders are committed by someone who stole the weapon. It might surprise some people that guns weren't always registered in this country. I believe that registering guns began in the 1970s. Before gun owners were required to register their firearms, people just didn't kill others at the rate they do now. Believe it or not, there was a time that schools didn't require resource officers either. Since there was a time that no one registered their guns and there was no school shooting, it makes one think that it's not the gun that's evil, it's the person who decided to point the gun at another fellow human being. Again, I ask. How does registering a firearm prevent evil? This makes me conclude that making gun laws does not help stop evil.

So what I'm suggesting is that there needs to be a serious look at what has caused our society to become so calloused about disrespecting other fellow human beings. If you don't look at the cause and effects of any behavior, then it will continue, or maybe even get worse. I believe until this happens, no amount of gun control is going to change or stop evil. Also, until the laws that already exist are enforced, then all violence will continue. Anyone who commits mass killings should have to spend the rest of their lives behind bars without the chance of parole. Also, the insanity plea should not be an excuse for evil. Mental illness doesn't make a person evil. If the government agencies don't severely punish mass murders, then it's not hard to predict what to expect in the future on gun violence crimes.

During a time when gun violence was rare and everyone owned a gun, if not maybe several guns, we didn't have resource officers in schools, and families made sure their children were raised in a manner that contributed to society. It's sad today that most children are raised by the government in so many ways. Also, the courts along with the government decide how you should treat your children. I'm not saying that there wasn't room for improvements, but parents have lost almost all their rights to freely discipline in the way they need to in order to raise a halfway decent responsible adult. I also believe that today's children are lacking a proper upbringing because of fathers being absent from their lives, too much nonsense being taught in education, and the so-called social programs. Another problem is that courts are too involved in telling families how to raise children. Just think. When did people start having problems with their children being involved with the courts? There used to be maybe one program that housed youthful offenders, but now, there are too many to count. I remember when fathers were the judge, jury, and executioner when children misbehaved, and therefore, children learned that it didn't pay to misbehave. I remember the only time one of us got in trouble with the law. My brother and some of his friends thought it was cute to pull stop signs down, and the sheriff brought the little criminal back to my dad and told my father that he was sure that my father would take care of the problem. I'm not sure what happened to my brother, but the sheriff didn't ever have to deal with my brother again. Today, if a child gets into trouble, the whole system gets involved and makes it worse. I'm telling you when you see all these killing by young people, it's most likely result of too much government involvement and not enough parental involvement.

Other problems that have led to children being so-called mentally ill is Hollywood keeps making more and more garbage movies that reinforce that children don't have a time just to be kids. There are also people who want to educate little five-year-olds about sex. Why do they think little children should be bogged down with this information that they cannot fully process? Why do some people think you should talk to your children about all the social ills? As a child, one thing I disliked the most was listening to the news and adults talking. I really didn't think or care about politics until I was in my thirties. It seems to me that there is a time and a place for everything. I am convinced that I probably would have been mentally ill or suicidal if I had heard all that crap when I wasn't able to fully understand it anyway. It seems to me that people who insist children talk about things that they have no power over is more of an agenda than just educating a child about reality. Sometimes it's good to focus on positive things like teaching children right from wrong, or how they need to respect animals and other living things. Thank God that my parents didn't talk to us about adult problems.

You are probably wondering why I'm talking so much about why children should be protected from adult issues. Well, it's because children cannot, nor should they have to fix what they don't fully understand, nor is it their responsibility. I believe that talking about adult issues can cause a child to develop anxiety, depression, and this can cause a child to become a fearful neurotic adult. This is just to a few of the adverse effects that happens to children because they are forced to listen or learn about adult issues. They are not ready for all the crap that adults deal with, and most children don't have the intellectual ability to mentally or emotionally understand adult discussions. Overall, I believe that children can often develop a sense of being vulnerable and lack the ability to figure out how to help or change a given situation that is upsetting the adults. Example: it's just like the feeling most children get when one or both parents abandon them, or they perceive that they are the reason that their absent parent no longer visits them.

Then people blame the president for not condemning a group, or make it harder for people to obtain a gun. Are you serious that there's gun violence because of it being the instrument that was used? What about the 18-wheeler that was used to kill or maim people in France? Did the 18-wheeler just decide to start up by itself? Please think outside the box because people are the ones who decide to kill, not the instrument. Again, until people in power realize this, innocent people will continue to die. Listen, it takes two mentally healthy adults to raise mentally healthy children and that's a parent's job. Of course, children can go against what they were taught, but usually, adults that kill other people just because they feel like killing someone is due to drug use. Not only the use of street drugs causes mental illness, but the use of street drugs takes away a person's consciousness, or drug use can block all reasoning, or masks emotions. One for the biggest problem today is that a lot of children are not being taught personal responsibility, nor are they learning empathy. People children treat others better when they are taught by example, or taught to treat others with respect. Just some thoughts.

Socialism or Controlism

Why on Earth would people want the government to take care of them? For the life of me, I don't understand people, which includes me. Most people think that there is something better. Unfortunately, any and all situations you can imagine has its drawbacks or downside. When analyzing any issue, I like to first decide what I think are the positives and then I try to decide what the negatives aspects most likely will be part of any give consequence or outcome. Sometimes it's hard to decide because I add an emotional component to the mix instead of thinking with a pragmatic component. I'm convinced that these two decision characteristics are what makes the difference between a good or bad leader. When a person makes decisions with an emotional component, then it usually doesn't get the problem solved. Usually if a person makes a decision based on using the pragmatic consideration, then a decision usually turns out better. I can't think of any situation that has only positive consequences or only negative results. In fact, the atomic universe works on mostly positive and negative components. You might agree or disagree, but in order to convince me, you'll need to come up with at least three examples where this law doesn't apply.

Now let's look at what some people see as positives of socialism and then we will look at the negatives, but keep in mind, I might not include all aspects of socialism because I'm not trying to write a book on socialism. I'm just pointing out what I see as positive and negative about this political viewpoint. Also, I find that a positives and negative consideration can overlap, or become blurred together. This can happen because some people think so differently that negatives might be positive and some positives might be negative. First, everyone is supposed to get free college, sounds great, but not everyone wants to go to college. In today's society, getting a degree isn't learning about different people opinions. Instead, college is becoming a tool to indoctrinate people into thinking alike. Higher education is supposed to be a learning experience that only happens by discussing and exchanging ideas that can help and/or solve various issues.

Free housing. This also sounds great because rent can be a problem, and landlords can raise the rent at will. My advice is try to purchase your own home because when the government provides free housing, then the government becomes your landlord and can limit your freedom, and they can dictate what you can or can't do in your own home. Just imagine or think what might happen if you don't comply. Who will be able stop the government from putting cameras in your home to keep control of every aspect of your life? Just some thoughts.

Free money. (Because you won't have to work, it won't be necessary.) What a concept. If one doesn't work, then what will they be doing to feel a sense of purpose? Personally, I like to work at a job of my choice and spend my money as I choose. Again, you can't predict what the government might decide to do after they give you free money. In fact, just think about how some of these politicians think about what they determine is not good for you. Think about how they might limit your choices, or how they believe people should live. Socialists believe that children should be parented by the government, and they want to be involved in people's lives from birth to death. It's not hard to believe that socialism will turn our government into ruling and becoming like China. In China, they tell parents how they can parent, or they might take your kids after two years of age and experiment on how to mold children into what the government wants or needs in order to maintain power. Wait! Our government already tells parents how to raise their children. Believe it or not, there was a time that parents could raise their children without government intervention, and they did just fine. In fact, they even did better. It's my opinion that a lot of social problems stem from government telling parents how to raise children. In a socialist government, your children may even get taken out of the home. They can and will take children if they decide that the parents are unfit, negligent, or maybe the parent isn't complying with their rules.

Another bad and one of the worst government ideas was to turn the education institutes into teaching children more about social justice instead of focusing on making sure no students leave high school who can't read and no students would graduate without being able to do at least basic math. Hopefully, most graduates have learned to think critically. Of course, some children do not have the ability to learn some things, but this is the exception, and it would help teachers if primary grades classrooms were limited to no more than twenty students.

You might have noticed by now that the government isn't really your big brother or friend, but the government wants to make sure that they survive and maintain control of every aspect of people's lives. What better way is there to control people than socialism? In fact, if you trade your liberties under capitalism for socialism, then it's like giving a rapist a gun and a victim. As you can imagine, there will be no limits on what the government does or doesn't do. They will not hesitate how they use their power or how far they will go to maintain that power. Just look at the way the democrats and some republicans have threated President Trump, and Trump's a powerful person himself. Look at how the radical antifa group has been allowed to get by with assaulting others under the guise of protesting. This group is being funded by powerful anti-Trump people and being ignored by anti-Trump media and lawmakers. My belief is that you might not like a person, but what's happening to President Trump and his supporters is not right morally or legally. Just ask yourself, "What if I or my family upset these powerful people, and they want to come after me?" Who is going to stop them from destroying you or your family's lives or reputations?

Basically, the rule of law in this capitalist country is supposed to help prevent abuse by government agencies or others from interfering in people's lives. Under socialism, which is more of the lawmakers in the democrat majority has embraced, they will abuse power even more than what they do now. When did it become okay not to allow a person due process, or to charge some with something that isn't even in the law books. It seems hard to believe or understand that democrats have decided they are going to impeach President Trump without any due process and they use hearsay as evidence. If they can be allowed to do this to President Trump, then what do you really think that they wouldn't come after the rest of us poor souls if they deemed it necessary? You would have no chance of escaping their abuse. I'm hoping that most people will listen to reason because once socialism takes root in America, you will be at the mercy of any person in power, and most likely, you will not be able to turn back the tide of socialism.

Last, I would like to know. Why don't people who like and want to live under socialism just move to a socialist country and let those of us continue to enjoy our freedom under a capitalist country? After all, America is the only capitalist country that provides so many freedom for its people. Therefore, it only seems fair that people who love capitalism should have a country in which they can live and enjoy freedom. A place where the people have more power than the government, and the government isn't in control. Also, a place where there is a rule of law that maintains and provides a basis for a civil society. A lot of people view the rule of law as the foundation of what makes this country so great. It is my strongest belief that socialism is nothing more than a way for powerful people to control others while benefiting themselves. Socialism is a sure way to give people power over your decision, and you need to understand that you will be at the mercy of people who will use and abuse their power. People will not be able to object to anything that the powers to be deem necessary in order to maintain control. You might say that it's capitalism that creates powerful people, which is true to some extent, but it's the constitution that provides parameters. With these parameter, the constitution provides the blueprint that assures Americans that they will be able to maintain the rights to be free and to live as they choose. You might think you have it bad now. Just wait and see what the results are after America becomes a socialist country. Then it will be too late. Also, I want to encourage everyone to make sure that before they vote, they think or read about how the Soviet Union's leader Stalin treated the people. Just some thoughts.

Taxation With or Without Representation

Taxes produce revenue for government, or are taxes a revenue for the politicians? It's hard to understand how so many politicians become wealthy when taxes are usually earmarked for specific needs or projects that are usually voted and agreed on by both chambers of the house. Yet they keep running out of money. Social security taxes are taken out of everyone's paycheck, but the government claims that social security is going bankrupt. Same thing with gas taxes. Each time you buy a gallon of gas, around fifty cents goes toward road repair and road maintenance. But again, the people who are supposed to manage this money have a hard time repairing the roads due to lack of money.

I figured that there is probably, each day in most states, at least two million gallons of gas being sold. That means that each state department of transportation is getting at least one million dollars or more per day to pay for repairing and maintaining safe roads. How is it possible that there are potholes that don't get repaired for weeks if not months or years? This makes one ask, "Is there anyone auditing how gas taxes are spent?" And if not, they need to hire a group of private citizen to do an audit every month. Also, I think it would be a good idea to hire private companies to do some of the roadwork. Private companies can probably do just as good of a job, and the price would be less than what government workers get paid, and they might even do a better job. Anyway, tax dollars or tax-paid services shouldn't be used by government workers or agencies to prosper from and/or a way for them to enrich their bank accounts. Just some thoughts.

Another complaint that I have against people in government, especially democrats, is about taxes. It seems that government officials never get enough taxes, and they always find some new way to tax a person. My thought is why not have a flat tax that everyone has to pay for, which is fair and equal. This would provide a way for every person to contribute, and it is a way that doesn't punish someone just because they are rich. Of course, the people on a fixed income should be exempt.

Next, once the lawmakers pass a fair tax bill, then they should think about getting rid of pork barrel projects. There are plenty of people in the private sector who probably believe in these projects and would be happy to donate and can feel good about themselves and give them a sense that they are making a difference. It just seems to me that if taxpayers are paying for these projects, then they should have a say whether they want to pay for studying why chimpanzees throw their feces. Personally, I think that all animals do what they do because they are laying down boundaries for other animal to respect. This study might be interesting for some people, but it isn't anything that will benefit most taxpayers. Another area where taxpayers shouldn't have to pay taxes is if another person wants to have a medical procedure done that is not necessary for sustaining life. Example: it would probably boost my self-esteem if I could get a tummy tuck, or other plastic surgery, but that's not how tax dollars should be spent. I have every right to save money until I can pay a specialist in this area to do my tummy tuck.

The taxpayers should make sure that government officials are held accountable for any misuse of tax dollars, or any abuse of continually raising taxes. Also, tax dollars should only be used for what they were intended, and earmarks or pork barrel projects should only be paid from taxes if it benefits the American citizens. Social security monies should only be used for paying social security benefits. Gas taxes should be used for keeping the roads maintained and repairs. Otherwise, it's like me telling the IRS that I'm going to send them my taxes, then turning around and use the money for relocating in a different country. Corruption comes in many forms, but the result usually is the same. Just some thoughts.

Last, the government should not be able to raise taxes on a person's property just because they can. This is wrong, and people shouldn't have to pay more taxes whenever the government decides that they need more money. Property tax should be kept to a reasonable amount that give the owner the most benefit. Also I'm against the estate tax. If a person has worked hard and invested that money to benefit their heirs once they die, the government should not ever be allowed to steal it from the grieving families. The person who dies should be able to pass it on to someone whom they want to inherit their lifetime accumulation of material goods. After all, they worked, and they already paid taxes yearly on their property as will the ones who inherits the property. This amounts to taxation upon taxation, which should be illegal. When the government decides they have the right to take property for taxes, then it's just a fancy way to get away with robbing a person and not having to face the consequences. Also, it's a crime of opportunity and vulture like behavior. I tell you, if the government could figure out how to tax people for breathing air, they would, and they probably would figure out a way to disconnect or justify, not allowing you to live. So until the hardworking patriots get and keep politicians in office who have a better moral compass, then it will continue unchecked. Just some thoughts.

Them versus Us

America, like any other country, has problems but that is because people are in control, and when people are in control, there will always be problems of various origins. But it doesn't help when some people want to dwell on the past. The past is the past, and the current population didn't participate in the injustices of past times. Besides that, all whites didn't own slaves, nor did all whites hate Native Americans. In fact, my Irish great-grandfather married a Native American. It seems to me that people who use past wrongs are just trying to be manipulative and blame their problems on someone or something else. For example: Black Lives Matter can go around threatening to kill cops, and some do kill police officers, yet they cry that they are being mistreated. Maybe the next time you need help with an emergency, you'll think twice about calling the police because you hate them. Listen, I don't think anyone likes to get a ticket or go to jail, but if this nation went back to the Wild West type of justice, a lot of people would be begging for the return of law and order. Personally, when I was in a bad car accident, it was the first responders that helped save my life. Blacks and other minorities have agencies to fight the system. Whites never did have anyone to fight their battles and learned to think and do for themselves. Also, it helps to have a good work ethic. Although that isn't always the case in today's social culture.

I've just been around a few blacks, but they seem like decent people who are no different from myself, except they are darker. They want to work and raise their children in an environment that is safe and one that doesn't have a lot of crime and drama. Personally, I think most people when given a chance want this also. I've always thought that people have more in common than difference regardless of skin color. This is why America is so great. It's the land of opportunity, and if you choose not to take advantage of our freedom to better your circumstances, then it's not because you are black. Rather, it's because you decided that you don't have to do anything more than complain and blame the white people. Then people will feel guilt and give you excuse after excuse why you are stuck in poverty and you can justify your behaviors toward police and blame others.

Although I see some very successful blacks on various talk shows and sports, I'm not jealous. They have more money and power than I've ever obtained, yet they continue to complain, and they still keep complaining about white privilege. My belief is no matter what you do, some people will never be happy. This makes me believe one or two things that causes such prejudices. Either they are jealous of what the whites have accomplished, or they have a deep irrational fear of not being as good as the white people. Of course, they are just as important as other people, but they just benefit too much from certain talking points. Seems to me some people feel better about themselves by blaming others. I'm white, but I don't see that I'm privileged, nor are most the whites that I know. In fact, I never have met a white supremacist either and tend to think that this boogey-man theory is just another way to not have to play by the same rules as other folks. Some people want to be special and expect others to handle them with kid gloves. The only population that should be considered as special is the developmentally delayed people.

The difference between successful people and the unsuccessful is not the color of a person's skin. What is the problem though is people who have the attitude that someone owes them. Why don't you just figure out what the attitude is for people who are successful instead of whining about others? Just maybe you will be able to find a way that will give you a pathway to better finances. Then someone will complain about you having more. The people that I've known that are financially successful are the ones who planned their lives, sacrificed, and worked hard to achieve their goals. One last thought. If we are to all get along in this country, we all need to see each other as people instead of seeing people based on what group or skin color. Last, to continue down the road of blaming others for your misfortune is to travel a road to self-destruction and misery. Just some thoughts.

Toxic Masculinity or Toxic Stupidity

It just boggles my mind why some people think that men and women are equal in any way shape or form. The only exception might be that they both can be capable of great good or some can be capable of great evil. Otherwise I don't think that one should compare themselves to others. It seems to me that people might be jealous or maybe they don't believe that women are physically weaker of the two sexes. I say this because I'm a fairly strong women, but I know by experience that all eight of my brothers and all three of my sons were a lot stronger. In all my years I've never had a need to compete with males. Although, due to small class sizes, when I was in middle school the girls and boy played sports together.

It seems to me that because we are born physically different than it's just logical to believe that males and females are different and not equal. If you think about how everyone on this planet have different finger prints and DNA that is unique. Hopefully this fact might help you understand that just because you want to be equal, doesn't make it so. Why are so many people hung up on the equality between the sexes? Personally, I have no problem with men being masculine in fact I'm glad that I haven't had to do some of the things that men do quite easily. So I believe that this is just another attempt for people to make a society that they think is best for this country. They don't stop and think that maybe some women like the fact that they can depend on a man who is physically stronger, aren't whiners nor complainers, and they like to be protectors.

Next, Instead of trying to change men, maybe some women should look at their toxic behavior. It all comes to the understanding that we can try to change others, but it's a lot easier to change oneself. Also, some women just don't like men or maybe they just have had a father that made them feel bad about themselves. My advice to these women would be that it's best not to judge all men because of past bad experiences from men. I believe that when someone is trying to control others or they want to change them for whatever reason, it tells me that they don't like thinking about their own behavior. Also controlling behavior can be a form of narcissistic behavior and they are just not able to look at their own flaws. These types of people whether male or female usually are very critical of others. Therefore it's not so much about equality, but rather it's about controlling unhappy people.

One difference that I've noticed about some women is they tend to try and change their husbands into someone that they are not. It almost seems to me that these women would prefer someone else. It is my belief that all people should make sure that they critique their own behavior and maybe once in a while even suggest to others how their behavior affects them, but it's better to just accept their flaws until that person realizes a need for change. I'm not talking about accepting any abuse from a man, but rather maybe just realizing that men look at things different than women. It's ok for both men and women to bring out the best in each other, but some women want to change their significant other completely. I believe both the men and women should try to focus on appreciating their significant others positive attributes.

Another thought concerning toxic masculinity. I'd rather have men around that are protective and pragmatic, than one who creates a lot of drama. I believe for whatever reason that more females are bossy and they can nag or complain about everything. Women like this are usually very unhappy and they tend to think that they are better than men. Men who are in a relationship with these types of women will never be able to prove themselves worthy in this relationship.

Next, just stop and think what would happen if a group of mostly men came to conquer this country and there were no more masculine men who see their jobs as protectors. Do you really believe that those foreign invaders are going to worry about your rights? Women do you really believe that other masculine men from some of these other countries would worry about your equal rights? Do you think that these men would ask you about your feelings? My advice is to stop complaining about men and realize that women have their own behaviors that can be just as upsetting to men. I'm not sure what type of person sits around thinking about how to change everyone else but themselves. But it's really scary to think about how many people join in and support these types of people.

Here is an example of a women who complained about prayer in the schools. I know this isn't about masculinity, but in essence it shows what can happen when people try to change others. I remember hearing about a lady named Madeline O'Hare who decided to complain about prayer in schools. Keep in mind that she was an atheist, so anything to do with God probably was offensive. She actually was able to get enough people to listen to her and she won the case against prayers in schools. It is hard to understand because during that time most people in the United States believed in God. How does anyone convince others to get rid of anything that isn't causing harm to the majority? Again, Madeline O'Hare actually accomplished getting prayers taken out of school. It just goes to prove that even one person can change the attitude of a society and it's not always a good change. Also, she didn't necessarily understand what the consequences might end up being. It seems though that the consequences for Madeline O'Hare might have been different and she might have even lived a longer more productive life if she had just determined to live and let live. But it all came full circle when years later her skeletal remains were found under her home. If I remember correctly, it was her youngest son who had killed her. My advice ladies, just treat your sons and husbands, not as projects to change, but rather let them just be men who will use their masculinity to protect those they love. One last thing, if you need a project in changing someone, look into a mirror, and just enjoy being a woman who has potential to do great things. I find that making sure I'm a good person is a big job that never ends. Just some thoughts.

Trump Derangement Syndrome

Since the 2016 election, it is obvious that the left-leaning politicians and their dishonest media has spewed so much hate about Trump. It's obvious that these same people have developed so much hate for Trump, Trump's family, and anyone who likes him that some are exhibiting signs of mental illness. At first, I thought it was just hate that sooner or later would subside, but three years later, the Trump haters are not able to see that they are being irrational. They even project their behaviors and thoughts onto Trump, and they even regress into a mindset of a child. It's quite alarming how off the chart that the left and their minion's behavior is toward President Trump. What they accuse him of is what they are doing themselves. One example is when they group together and try to bully him into doing what they think. Talk about bullies. I've never seen such animosity directed to anyone, and it's just because they hate him.

I have tried to understand why the left hates President Trump, but I haven't come up with a very good reason other than that they feel threatened that he isn't one of them. So I've decided to show and explain to you what I believe is the problem. Keep in mind, though, that I have no inside information, but I have been analyzing the behaviors of the people who have irrational hate toward President Trump. What I'm about to write about is my opinion from what I've observed. I'm not accusing anyone specifically for any wrongdoing, but rather, I'm trying to explain the depth and length of what Trump haters will or might do in order to destroy anyone they see as a problem. It's not a far or outlandish comment when I say, "If they would treat a president the way they have, then what do you think might happen to everyone else from whom they feel threatened?"

One thing that I noticed when Trump was running for president was that people who used to like him thought it was funny and that Trump running for President was just a joke. They just knew that he couldn't possibly have a chance to become the next president of this great country. As time went on, and Trump won the Republican primary, these so-called friends began to show their true colors. This, I believe, is when the progressive segment in this country started getting worried that Trump might just have a good chance of becoming the next president. Of course, there were some who still laughed at this possibility and thought it was just a joke. The democrats and their followers just couldn't or wouldn't accept the possibility that Trump could win. After all, Hillary Clinton was destined to become the first female president. Therefore, there was no way that she would fail to secure the election on November 5, 2016.

In the meantime, Trump kept going to various states to campaign, and he always drew massive crowds wherever he went. This should have been a big clue for the progressives, but because they were too smart to be wrong and that there was no way that Trump would win, therefore, there was nothing for them to worry about. This type of thinking continued until the day of the 2016 election. Then the unthinkable happened, and their worst nightmare unfolded before their very eyes. Trump had secured the election because he received the most electoral votes. This sent them into a state of shock that they never would get over, nor were they ever going to accept Trump being their president. Since they weren't going to accept the results, they decided to start the anti-Trump smear campaign. So all of the progressive media, all of the progressive politicians, and even some Never Trumpers couldn't stop Trump from becoming the forty-fifth president of the United States. What a blow to their egos. This is where the left-leaning people and their minion's hate began to blossom into Trump Derangement Syndrome. Once Trump secured the 2016 election, and the shock and disappointment of Hillary not securing the election, just drove them over the edge. How could people who used to like him become so hate filled? I believe the answer is that these people knew that Trump would not be someone who could be easily pushed around. After the election, you could see just how unhappy and threatened by President Trump winning had affected them. I believe, also, that some of the people who hated the election results began to realize just how it might change how business is done on Capitol Hill.

Next, once Trump was sworn in, and the progressive's worst fears were realized, it was apparent that they needed to devise a plan to invalidate the election and one that would make sure that Trump never severed in any way or capacity for any government office. It's my belief this plan also was a way to make sure that no one else would dare to go up against the swamp. It's always been my belief and my observation that people who experience fear, hate, and jealousy can become consumed with these emotions, and they can become capable of doing anything that is necessary to destroy whoever or whatever is the object of their hate. Although most people have experienced these emotions of fear, hate, and jealousy, most people will get rid of these destructive feeling so that they don't become unhinged and do something they regret. You can see how these emotions if left to fester can drive people into doing much harm to even President Trump. The way that some actors talked and suggested that they would like to see Trump dead is one example of how hate can cause harm to others. It's hard to believe or even imagine why anyone would hate Trump just because he was elected the forty-fifth president of the United States of America. What was he supposed to do? Should he have just laughed and said, "I'm really not interested in the job?"

Again, it is my belief that there can only be one reason for such a drastic change in the way they felt toward Trump. This change happened because they knew and realized that Trump wouldn't be doing business like other politicians and, therefore, presented a threat to exposing or getting in the way of how things are done in Washington, DC. This became the point where panic and fear drove the progressives into colluding a way to make sure that Trump wasn't president for long. They decided to move to plan B, and this is where their agenda to get the election overturned was solidified.

The way I believe that the swamp creatures within the intel and the law enforcement agencies decided to devise a plan that would look like the Russians interfered with our election, and Trump was colluding with them so that he could win the election of 2016. Thus, the Russian interference into our election was given for the reason why Trump had won the election. This plan became the powerful tool that was used by the intel community to convince and/or manipulate the voters into believing that Trump only became president because he was colluding with Russia. Therefore, there needed to be a special counsel appointed to look into how Trump and the Russians were able to steel the presidency from Hillary Clinton. This is where the plan became a team effort to bring Trump down and to delegitimize his presidency. On the downside for the president was that even people who used to be his friends hated him, and he probably knew that the special counsel would probably not give him a fair break. Therefore, the progressives would use any means necessary to bring him down, and they would use any means necessary to convince the American people that they were just misguided by Trump. This is where they were convincing themselves and justifying why he was the enemy and had to be taken down by the so-called honest people in order to save this country. This is why there was a decision to make it look like Russians and candidate Trump colluded to interfere with Hillary becoming the president of the United States.

I believe that the way the intel and FBI could make sure that this Russian collusion was real and necessary was to create a path in the computer that showed some type of Russian interference. The way they might have accomplished this is by using a specific computer app that allowed them to make it look like the Russians had put information into our computer systems. I understand that these agencies have a way to send a communication from one computer in one country or state and make it look like it's from another state or country. I'm not saying that I know this for a fact, but I believe it could have possibly been what happened. Otherwise, why do so many in congress believe that the Russians really were involved? Also, this was the first time in my life that anyone has ever mentioned

Russian interference in our elections. Who knows just how much misinformation is given to the American people.

Finally, the results of the 2016 presidential election, I believe, consumed the hate-filled swamp creatures, and it just wasn't any option for them to accept the results. They couldn't believe or explain how so many people could even vote for Trump. The only explanation that could possibly explain these voters' support for Trump was that they must be just a bunch of ignorant deplorable people who needed to be taught a lesson. This lesson was a way to teach them about what happens to people when they don't think or believe like the powerful swamp creatures. Even after plan B failed, the swamp creatures had to devise another lie in order to continue the quest of keeping the status quo of the powerful swamp people that exist in the government. The swamp creatures who want to be able to control this country no matter what the American people think or who they vote into office. This, folks, is why it's crucial for the taxpayers to make sure that they get out and vote. Just some thoughts.

World Peace

Almost everyone wants and deserves to live in a peaceful environment, but is that possible? Each of us has our own version of what it would be like to live in a world where there would be no hate and everyone got along. This would be away to create an atmosphere of joy and positivity for everyone and life would be problem free. Also, most of us have an opinion on how world peace might be accomplished and what the world could accomplish if people could learn to get rid of hate and learn to live peacefully with others regardless of our differences. It seems like a noble concept, but is world peace obtainable? Just understanding human behavior will give most people an insight into just how difficult it is for even two people to find peace all the time. Some people can't even find peace with themselves. Although I can't imagine why anyone would not want to be at peace and live a stress-free life, I equally can't imagine how anyone thinks that peace is actually possible. I hate to be the one to say this, but because people have the ability to be either good or evil, I believe it just isn't going to happen in this life. It's been my experience that it takes a lot of soul searching and determination not to repay evil for evil, and I think more people than not have this problem. If it wasn't for the laws that are in place, we'd all realize that we are all capable of retribution if we decided to act on our thoughts.

One may be at peace with themselves, but just add another person in your environment, and it's guaranteed that somewhere in that relationship, there are going to be conflicts. You might have already guessed where I'm going with this thinking. The more the merrier may be accurate for a moment in time, but the more interaction that people are involved in a home, county, city, state, or country, the more chances of disagreement. Also, it's guaranteed that hurt feelings or other emotions will arise in relationships of all forms regardless of how much you think that you can accomplish world peace. My experience is where you find humans, you might find peace for a moment, but because we are all flawed creatures, we will sometimes get upset or irritated with others.

Again, it would be nice to have peace everywhere, but is that realistic? Personally, I don't like the thought of war, but since the beginning of time, people don't seem to know how to live peacefully with others. I'd say in some situations, you can learn to be peaceful, but there's not a place in the world that is free of all conflict. Families who love one another have moments of wanting to hurt the other person and most of the time feel that they have a very good reason why that person is wrong.

Why do we think that we can be friends with everyone if we learn that it's just a matter of loving others? This is just not true. Even I don't like some people regardless of culture. In fact, even people of my own culture may not be someone I like. Does that make me a horrible person? I don't think so. I'm a person who likes to be around other people but don't like being around people who are rude, destructive, negative, or get high on drugs. Also, I think it's hard for anyone to be around violent, self-serving people who don't think about how their behaviors affect others. I'm sure that not everyone likes me and that's okay. Why do some people think that everyone should like them, and if they don't like them, then it must be that they are bigots? My advice is, don't worry about what others think and find friends that value you as a person. It's my opinion that if someone doesn't like me, then they have every right to leave me alone and not be around me, and I sure don't want to be around them. Can they be a bigot and dislike me because I'm white, possibly, but that's even okay unless they are trying to cause me personal harm or do harm to my family, In fact, if they just live and let live, they will probably find that life is more peaceful.

When I hear someone say let's just get to know one another and understand them, I think to myself, *Does that mean that as long as I think and behave like the rest of the group, then I'll be more acceptable?* This is not possible because we all have experienced life differently, and the environment we grew up in has a lot to do with how we view things differently. Getting to know others can help people get along but getting along depends on many factors. Personally, I don't expect people to agree with everything that I think, and I'm always going to question anything that I don't believe or understand. Of course, most people naturally like to have people reaffirm them, but in today's society, you are expected to think just like everyone who thinks that they know best. If you don't, then you are called various names. What type of person thinks you have to agree with their thinking all the time in order for you to be acceptable? Why are people bigots just because they disagree? Is this what some consider living in peace? I call this type of thinking as being narrow-minded and manipulative.

To me, living in a world where there is peace means that you should live and let live. Accept that people might have a lot in common, but there will be times of disagreements, which is okay, and we all need to respect others' opinions. I'm not saying that we have to accept that person view on life, but we don't have the right to interfere in their lives, or call them names either.

Next, laws are guidelines that help people to maintain a more peaceful society, and most people who learn to comply with these laws usually have a more peaceful life. I can say with certainty though that without laws, there most likely would be less peace and more crime. What I do believe though is when people start talking about changing freedom of speech so that you don't offend others doesn't necessarily provide a peaceful climate. Who's to say what speech is good and which isn't good? I'm sure that discussion would not remain peaceful. So let's forget about trying to monitor someone else's behaviors. I don't agree with monitoring others speech because this is just another way for people to tell others how to live. Again, if you don't like the way a person talks or behaves, then don't associate with them. I believe that everyone has the right to do and say what they want as long as it's not being forced on someone else. Of course, there are words and phrases that I don't say but that doesn't mean that I should tell others how to conduct their lives. It might help bring about world peace if everyone would just live and let live. Why don't everyone just monitor their own behavior instead of trying to change others? Of course, you can communicate to others your dislikes, but in order to keep the peace, it might be better to live and let live.

My advice is that it's probably a better idea to leave people live with their own decision as long as they aren't committing a crime against person or property. Of course, you need to consider the person and situation, but I never want to become a controlling phony. Also, how you talk might offend me. Are you willing to change and include yourself in getting rid of some of your speech that offends me? I don't like the way a lot of people use the F word. How many people will be willing to stop saying that word just because I'm offended? Do you see my point? Why should I change my speech, and you don't do the same? Maybe you should look at your own hateful speech and behaviors you have toward people whom you disagree. I'm sure you wouldn't like it either. Just try being open-minded and realize that people can still live at peace with one another as long as people don't try to force their own thinking as what is best for everyone.

Last, if you really believe in peace and understand that people think and sometimes view things differently, then you need to understand that a peaceful society has to develop parameters and boundaries that maintain order. This is why it is necessary to make laws and have consequences that is beneficial for everyone. Laws, when followed by most people, will help any society get along, and people will usually learn to live peacefully together. Of course, each person should respect that others have a right to live without being harassed. Also, those in power need to respect the rights of the people that are in this country. These rights are outlined in the constitution of this country. The constitution gives us a guide of how to live a free, productive life. I truly believe that without laws that our freedom would be limited and a peaceful life would be next to impossible. Just some thoughts. Of course, laws and lawmakers need to agree with the precepts of the Constitution of the United Sates.

White Privilege

Let's look at some terminology or maybe dissect what white privilege means to me. In order to do this, we need to look up each word that is associated with the social context as well as the literal meaning. If a person knows the literal meaning, then they can have a basis to judge and insert their own thinking. Therefore, we can better judge for ourselves how the overall meaning could be interpreted. Personally, knowing what I know about society and people, white privilege is meant as something negative. People who say white privilege are bigoted and this type of rhetoric is meant to stir up trouble and to divide for political purposes. It's hard for me to fully understand anyone wanting to divide a country because it usually leads to a bloody conflict or war. Who in their right mind wants people to get killed? After all, it might be someone they care about or maybe even themselves who gets badly injured or killed. After all, there are a lot of culturally blended families. Instead of trying to foster hate, all Americans should strive toward ways to live in peace. But, of course, it's up to each individual to do their part in helping maintain the peace in this country. Also, instead of looking at what others are doing or what some have done in the past, one could better serve their country by looking at how they can contribute in some positive manner.

White is a color that describes a Caucasian person, or it can be associated with clouds, etc.

Privilege means a right or munity granted as a peculiar benefit, advantage, or favor.

Peculiar means different from the usual or normal; characteristic of only one person, group, or thing.

Prejudice is an irrational attitude of hostility directed against a group, race, or their supposed characteristics.

Now that we have an idea of what the meaning of the words white, privilege, prejudice, and peculiar mean, we can maybe better understand and discuss the social context and the literal meaning for me and others.

To me, the social context of white privilege today is used to demean white people because they have been successful, and some groups of people can't handle that because they are either prejudice, fearful, and/or jealous. I realize that a long time ago some whites owned slaves, but it was a bunch of whites who fought and/or died to free the slaves. I'm sure that people will get anger, but today, it's not the whites that are the slavers; it's the people who hate the whites because they are slaves to their own hatred. Look, I'm not sure why people treat others so badly, but I do know that when you hate someone, you take a chance of becoming just like them or even worse. I believe people who hate others are just angry people. People who want to hang on to hate always want to blame someone else for their problems, and when people blame others, then they learn to justify their own evil behavior. You probably think you could never be like that person. I'm not saying that your feelings are invalid, but I do believe that anger and hate can lead to doing evil.

I know what you're thinking about me but hear me out. Although I'm not black, I grew up very poor. There wasn't a day that went by during the nine years that I attended school that someone would either make fun of me, or they excluded me from being part of an activity. I was made fun by kids and some adults, and it was all because I was poor. I don't go around hating people who have more or mistreat others who are less fortunate. In fact, I think and believe that God did me a favor because I'm not a person who hates anyone else, but on the other hand, I don't associate with those who do hate. Instead of letting a few evil, or misguided people live in your head, or your thinking, just try to focus on how you can benefit from capitalism and better yourself.

Last, I like to think that Martin Luther King was someone that was trying to bring people together, and he understood that hate breeds hate. The reason I've learned to turn the other cheek and why I remind myself not to repay evil for evil is because of people such as Jesus and Martin Luther King. Personally, I believe most people's reaction is to repay people for their hurtful behavior. It might help to ask yourself. Does repaying evil for evil make you a better person, or does it make you just as evil as the person you hate? Anyway, people of all cultures, beliefs, and backgrounds should just live and let live. Just some thoughts.

Instead of letting a few evil or misguided white people control your thinking and your behaviors, maybe it might help if you think about the positive attributes and the accomplishments that the white culture contribution that were positive for this country. Since you probably are having difficulty with this, let me provide a list of just a few positive things that mostly whites have contributed to the betterment of America.

1. The men who developed the constitution that gives us so many freedom and provides a blueprint or basis for laws that provide a better life for people. One thing I would like to mention now because some of these men owned slaves, which I believe was just how things back then were for the people in power. Do I think it was right? No, but I'm confident that not all slave owners were brutal or cruel. But the bottom line is no one knows but the people of that time and the good Lord in heaven. This, my friends, is where everyone will truly have to answer for how they treated others.

2. Taming the Wild West, agriculture, and other commerce that was necessary for becoming a free and prosperous country. It couldn't have been an easy job because there wasn't much of an infrastructure or modern conveniences. I'm not saying that other cultures didn't help, rather, just by the ratio of whites that lived in America can give you an idea that it was mostly whites.

3. There were many whites who fought and quite a lot of whites that died or were injured in the Civil War to free the slaves. I would think that people could understand from the sacrifice made by so many whites that it would make

a difference in how some blacks view most whites, but I believe that most people tend to look at the negative first and then if they want to make their lives better, they begin to focus on the positive attributes of others, or the situation with which they live.

4. More whites were involved in developing the industrial revolution, some important inventions like electricity and things like advances in science, just to mention a few. This happened because they were able to see in vision a need, and it had nothing to do with white privilege. I do believe that people who succeed do so because they take chances and work hard. I personally wished I could do something great to inspire or help people. It seems to me that there are plenty of black Americans that have overcome their circumstances. I'm not saying that blacks haven't been treated badly by people who are white, but they have not been treated badly by all whites because I, for one, don't like or dislike someone else due to factors other than how they behave and/or think about life. I don't like some white people who believe it's okay to go around harassing or causing trouble for others.

One last thought that all people could adopt in how they approach life. Everyone needs to remember or believe that all people are created in God's image; therefore, every human being has abilities, problems, hopes and dreams, and failures and demons that make them who they are and what they can become if they focus on the positive of human nature. I try not to judge anyone's soul, but I have learned the hard way that not everyone has good intentions; therefore, I learned to judge what those intentions might be from how they behaved.

One last comment about being rejected by people no matter the reason. Others have experienced rejection and cruelty from others that aren't black. Probably not to the same level, but some people can understand what that can do to a person. Just remember that you can choose to do better than cruel hateful ignorant people, or you can choose to be a better person who can care about others that are struggling. Another thing I can't stress enough is that you can't change others, but you can change yourself if you just forgive and forget the pathetic, miserable people who just have no ability to look within their souls to see, and they have no resolve to care about anyone but themselves. It is my true belief that until a person stops blaming others, they will never be able to look at themselves and move forward in becoming the best person they can be in a prosperous society. Just some thoughts.

About the Author

Kara More grew up in a mountain valley and was the next to the youngest of twelve children. Out of the twelve, she had eight brothers and three sisters of which were all older than her except one brother. All twelve of them had the same biological parents. Her dad worked as a farm/ranch hand, while her mom was a stay-at-home mom. She attended the first nine years of her education at a small school where the class size of at the most eighteen students and that was usually after two classes were combined. Although neither of her parents finished eighth grade, they were expected to do well in school and that included not getting into trouble. They knew from an early age what was expected when they didn't listen to their parents, so there was a big incentive to behave and to do well at school.

She remembers her mom being angry at her father and them kids, but she hardly ever used physical punishment. Although she threatened them on a regular basis with telling their dad after he got home. It was obvious that with their mom, they could get by with more but was careful not to give her a reason to inform their father. Although she wasn't the disciplinarian in the family, she had a regular routine, and they knew what she expected. She wasn't a very feminine woman, and she didn't present herself as a weak person. On the other side, her dad worked hard and would have no problem whipping their posteriors, or using various forms of nonphysical methods such as making them stand in a corner, but he never beat them, or used verbal anger during any times of discipline. He also didn't ask why they misbehaved but rather was very calm when administering the consequences or results of misbehaving. She never saw her dad show any anger that was over the top, and he mostly stayed calm.

Although her mom believed in God and reminded them of what their morals and manners should be in various situations, her dad was an atheist and didn't seem to be bothered by her mom's religious thinking. In fact, she never ever heard her father mention God except when he cussed, yet he let them attend church and celebrate Christmas. Nether of her parents drank alcohol or used any type of drugs except what was over the counter or various natural cures that her mother knew about. Her mom took care of all of the families' medical problems with various plants, or other herbs.

Her parents both were part Native American and part Irish. They taught them to have respect for other people especially their elders. They talked about and taught them to learn by natural consequences and taught them to take personal responsibility for their behavior. They were taught not only to respect people, but they also talked about respecting all forms of life. She'll never forget being told by her mom, "If you don't want the cat to scratch you, then don't pull its tail."

The Irish part of them was how they didn't cause problems for anyone unless they started the fight first. Her brothers had a saying, "Don't fight unless the other person starts it, and then if you decide to fight, you were expected to finish the fight." Also, they learned to say what they thought to the person in question. Of course, some of them were kinder about how they said it. One of her brothers' favorite saying was, "I won't start a fight, but I will finish the fight." Of course, the stubborn and determined side came from their Irish ancestors. She believes that their Native American ancestry is what gave them most of their intelligence because most of them don't know when to keep their opinions to themselves. Just some thoughts.

Last, she's an educated woman who has experienced a lot of various trials in life, which has made her a better person that tries to be understanding of others daily. She doesn't believe that judging others is her job and tries very hard not to judge others, but she does pick and chooses her friends. Her experiences with people, her observations of people's behaviors (including her own), and what she learned through her educational study is what has given her the ability to write on a variety of subjects that can and do affect most people within our society. With this in mind, she hopes whoever decides to read her opinions will understand that she's not trying to think she's smarter, but rather, just maybe she might have something of value to share.